A Practical Guide to

Information Systems Process Improvement

A Practical Guide to

Information Systems Process Improvement

Anita Cassidy
Keith Guggenberger

S^t_L

St. Lucie Press
Boca Raton • London
New York • Washington, D.C.

Library of Congress Cataloging-in-Publication Data

Cassidy, Anita
   A practical guide to information systems process improvement/ by Anita Cassidy
and Keith Guggenberger
      p.   cm.
      Includes bibliographical references and index.
      ISBN 1-57444-281-3 (alk. paper)
   1. Management information systems. 2. Information technology. I.
Guggenberger., Keith. II. Title.
T58.64. C37 2000
      658.4′038′011—dc21

00-009370
CIP

Visit the CRC Press Web site at www.crcpress.com

© 2001 by CRC Press LLC
St. Lucie Press is an imprint of CRC Press LLC

No claim to original U.S. Government works
International Standard Book Number 1-57444-281-3
Library of Congress Card Number 00-009370
Printed in the United States of America   4 5 6 7 8 9 0
Printed on acid-free paper

PREFACE

This book is founded on the belief that process management, process improvement, and process reengineering must extend beyond the traditional business areas of Quality, Manufacturing, and Engineering and must enter the area of Information Systems. While process improvement may have impacted many other areas of an organization, Information Systems is one of the last areas in business to implement these concepts, even though it may have the most to gain.

Process improvement is a strategy for reducing overall costs, shortening cycle times, and improving quality and user satisfaction. For companies to remain competitive and survive in our global marketplace, quality and process improvements must extend into the Information Systems organization. Unfortunately, process concepts and techniques are not well understood and practiced by information systems professionals.

Companies may refer to their Information Systems organization in many different ways, such as Data Processing, Information Resource Management (IRM), Management Information Systems (MIS), or Information Technology (IT). The description we have chosen to use in this book is Information Systems (IS).

Simply put, this book is about improving Information Systems. Since Information Systems is composed of processes, this book is about information systems process improvement. All organizations are attempting to improve their Information Systems organization in an attempt to obtain more value from their technology investments. Whether the effort is labeled process improvement or not, the bottom line is to improve the efficiency and effectiveness of Information Systems.

This book is organized into ten chapters that provide a step-by-step methodology to lead you through practical improvements in Information Systems. It simplifies process improvement so you can begin to improve immediately and begin the evolution to world-class processes. This book helps identify the processes by providing a framework of processes typically found in an Information Systems organization. It then presents a methodology to improve the processes. Many examples, checklists, and templates are provided to help begin and guide your efforts.

Chapter 1 introduces the concept of information systems process management. It provides definitions and discusses the application of process management to Information Systems. This chapter explains why process improvement is important to Information Systems. A process evolution is introduced to assist in moving from a firefighting organization to a world-class organization. Barriers to change and process improvement tools and methodologies are also discussed.

Chapter 2 provides an overview of process fundamentals. It identifies what a process is, who is involved in a process, and specific process characteristics. An overview of the process improvement seven-step methodology is provided.

Chapters 3 through 9 are dedicated to outlining each step of the methodology in detail. Chapter 3 starts the process improvement effort by identifying improvement goals. The chapter assists in identifying metrics to measure the overall efficiency and effectiveness of an Information Systems organization and implement a culture of continuous improvement. An information systems balanced scorecard and metrics evolution is introduced to measure the overall effectiveness and efficiency. Chapter 3 also discusses how to establish a team and develop a project plan for the improvement effort and helps build a business Case for Action explaining why the Information Systems organization will benefit from a process improvement effort.

Chapter 4 assists in identifying and documenting information systems processes. A framework of typical processes is presented, including the interfaces, description, benefits, and issues.

Chapter 5 helps prioritize processes and select those to begin improving. Several different approaches to prioritize processes are presented.

Chapter 6 provides guidelines on gathering information about the process selected for improvement, including how to map or flowchart the current process. A cross-functional flowchart is introduced which provides a useful method of diagramming the process. The chapter then provides assistance in analyzing the current process.

A plan to improve the selected process is developed in Chapter 7. Specific process objectives and metrics are determined. Baseline and benchmark information is obtained for the process. A Case for Action is developed to outline the need for the improvement.

Chapter 8 provides guidance through the design of an improved process. Information is provided for selecting a process owner and holding the brainstorming and design sessions. Specific design techniques are provided as well as best practices that may be considered in the design of the new process. Risks in the new process are analyzed and the design is validated. Finally, the development of the process documentation is discussed.

Chapter 9 assists in implementing the improved process while considering its impact on technology and people. This chapter discusses the impact on the culture of an organization when evolving and becoming process driven. There may be an impact on the organization, the skill-set of individuals, technology, and management culture. All of these factors are important to consider in the process evolution. Continuous improvement in an organization reflects the management philosophy, as the processes are only as good as the leadership behind the processes.

Finally, a summary and overview of the process improvement effort is provided in Chapter 10.

This book is intended for management and information systems professionals interested in improving their information systems environment. An in-depth or detailed knowledge of information systems technology and process methodology is not necessary to benefit from the material presented. A Chief Information Officer (CIO) or executive Information Systems management will find this book especially helpful as they lead the process improvement initiative in their organization.

We sincerely hope this book helps in your journey to building a world-class information systems environment. Good luck on your journey.

ACKNOWLEDGMENTS

We would like to thank the many people who helped us write this book. Foremost, we would like to thank our spouses and families for their patience and support while the book was in progress. Without the support of our family and friends, this book would not have been possible. Many people, including Dan Cassidy, Stephanie Renslow, Dan Christian, Cheryl Stepney, Jean Collins, and Jenny Johnson, assisted us by reviewing and providing input for this book. We would also like to thank the numerous people with whom we have worked over the years as they have helped shape and mold the ideas presented in the book. Finally, this book is dedicated to you, the reader, because YOU have the power to make a difference and improve your information systems processes.

Anita Cassidy
Keith Guggenberger

ABOUT THE AUTHORS

Anita Cassidy has more than 24 years of experience in Information Systems. She is President/CEO of Strategic Computing Directions Incorporated in Minneapolis, Minnesota, an executive information systems consulting company specializing in strategic planning, e-business strategy, information systems assessment, temporary leadership, and process reengineering (www.strategiccomputing.com). She has been Vice President and Chief Information Officer at a worldwide manufacturing company, Director of Information Systems at a medical device manufacturing company, and Director of several divisions of a Fortune 100 instrument engineering and manufacturing company. Ms. Cassidy has a Bachelor of Science degree from the University of Minnesota and has also attended St. Cloud State University. Ms. Cassidy has authored a book titled *A Practical Guide to Information Systems Strategic Planning* published by St. Lucie Press (1998).

Keith Guggenberger is currently Vice President of Information Services at Starkey Laboratories, a worldwide manufacturer of custom in-the-ear hearing aids. In this position, he leads Starkey's global initiatives in the areas of mainframe, telecommunication, network, and worldwide business systems. He joined Starkey in 1986 upon graduation from the University of Wisconsin-Stout with a degree in Industrial Technology and cooperative experience with IBM and 3M. Prior to his present position, Mr. Guggenberger was Director of Quality where he championed many Total Quality Management initiatives including ISO9001 certification, Baldrige assessments, and business process redesigns.

CONTENTS

1

INTRODUCTION TO IS PROCESS MANAGEMENT

"The most effective way to cope with change is to help create it."

L. W. Lynett

PROCESS MANAGEMENT

What is process management? Process management is the method used to implement and continuously improve how products or services are delivered. The function is performed at a predictable level of service, support, time, and cost. Process management organizes a group of functional activities into steps that are measurable, repeatable, and reliable. A process management mentality is a fundamental change or transcendence from the firefighting mode found in many Information Systems organizations.

The principles of process management and Total Quality Management (TQM) are shown in Figure 1.1 and include:

- **Continuous improvement.** Continuously improve the goods and services produced by the Information Systems organization; continuously expand and grow to create a new future. This is a continuous process as new technologies and approaches become available.
- **Management commitment.** Top management must be committed to the improvement of processes. According to Dr. W. Edwards Deming, 85 percent of quality problems lie within management control. Management must change the culture of the organization and create an environment where continuous improvement can

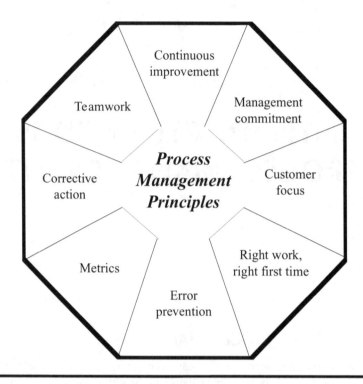

Figure 1.1 Process Management Principles

flourish. Management must also continually communicate their commitment, support, and interest.

■ **Customer focus.** Keep a customer focus at all times. Information Systems customers could be the internal customer or even the external customer. See the process through the eyes of the customer, not from the vantagepoint of Information Systems. The Internet and movement toward e-business are bringing information systems closer to the external customer. The objective is to establish a common definition of quality with the customer (either internal or external). Many different aspects and interfaces that the customer may have with Information Systems influence value and satisfaction. Some of the aspects a customer may consider when judging the quality of Information Systems include:

■ Time to get a request completed
■ Time to resolve a Help Desk call
■ System availability and up-time
■ System response time
■ Friendliness of personnel

- Knowledge of personnel
- Quality of the new system developed
- Accuracy of the information the systems produce
- Ability to utilize technology for a competitive advantage
- **Right work, right first time.** The goal for all activities is to do the right work and to do the work right the first time. Doing the right things includes obtaining the customers' true requirements. Doing the work right the first time includes both efficiency (little waste) and effectiveness (producing the desired results which include meeting or exceeding customer expectations).
- **Error prevention.** Errors can actually be prevented. Error-free work is always organized and planned with every activity, as it is always cheaper to do it right the first time. Rather than rewarding the heroic firefighter, reward those who actually prevent the fires from beginning in the first place. Ensure that processes have the necessary checks and balances to prevent errors. Anticipate that errors are going to happen before they actually happen. Analyze how you might be contributing to your own problems.
- **Metrics.** Processes and performance results are measured with specific metrics and targets. Positive trends exist for all measures.
- **Corrective action.** Problem solving is begun and corrective action is taken. The root cause of problems is determined, rather than just fixing the symptoms. When errors occur, rather than determining who made the error, the focus is on the problem correction and how the issue can be prevented in the future.
- **Teamwork.** Full teamwork is required to achieve improvements. Employee involvement, group brainstorming, and team efforts are common practices.

Process improvement includes technical aspects such as the tools, techniques, methodologies, and training. However, the behavioral aspects of process improvement must also be considered. These aspects include organizational issues, job responsibility changes, performance rewards, and culture as shown in Figure 1.2. Implementing a process mentality is a culture change for most Information Systems organizations. When working on processes, focus on both behavioral aspects and technical aspects.

BENEFITS OF PROCESS MANAGEMENT

Why is information systems process management important? What are the benefits? There are many benefits of implementing process improvement, such as:

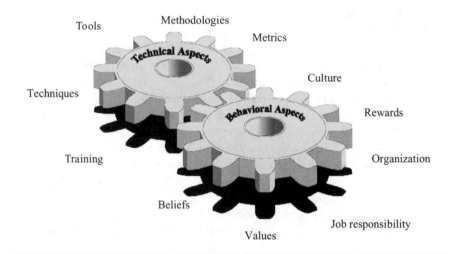

Tools   Methodologies   Metrics   Techniques   Culture   Rewards   Training   Organization   Beliefs   Values   Job responsibility

Figure 1.2 Process Improvement Aspects

- **Processes strengthen business partnership and improve customer service.** Improving information systems processes can result in a significant improvement of customer (or user) satisfaction, which in turn improves the relationship between the business and Information Systems. In this environment, Information Systems will be aligned with what is important to the business, and the priorities will be reflected in the day-to-day operations. The implementation of a quality initiative, or TQM, in the Information Systems organization can increase the value-added contribution to the organization. The Information Systems leader who speaks and embraces quality concepts can build bridges to other areas of the organization that have been using these techniques for years. Top management confidence in Information Systems will improve as the organization measures and improves the value it adds to the company.
- **Processes improve efficiency and communication.** Documented processes will clearly define roles and responsibilities of project team members. Knowing their job responsibilities and expectations will allow them to be more effective. Communication will be improved as responsibilities and expectations are clear and understood by everyone involved.
- **Processes improve productivity of the Information Systems organization.** For years, many businesses claimed that their Information Systems organizations were not responsive enough to changing business needs as they watched their backlog continue to grow. There are many examples of failed projects in the industry.

Many executives allege they spend too much money and time on projects that never meet business expectations. Information Systems is continually asked to do more with less. We all have limited budgets, limited headcount, and limited hours in a day. Rather than working harder, we need to find ways to work more productively. Process improvement can significantly improve and sustain new levels of performance and productivity.

■ **Processes improve effectiveness of project management.** Improved processes will assist Information Systems in consistently meeting commitments through better planning, estimating, costing, tracking, and reporting of project progress. Statistics from the Standish Group that studied 23,000 projects in companies of all sizes showed that in 1998 only 26 percent of projects were successful. They defined *successful* as completed on time, on budget, with the promised functionality. 46 percent of the remaining projects were challenged and 28 percent cancelled. As an industry, Information Systems professionals must improve the success rate of project development and project management. Becoming a process-based organization is one condition for consistently delivering successful projects.

■ **Processes reduce defects and improve quality.** Having a consistent and reliable process with metrics will provide the vehicle to improve and to increase the quality of service provided. Typically, the root cause of failure or defects is due to process and organizational failure, not failure of people.

■ **Processes help avoid bad publicity.** Today, system failures and system quality issues are highly publicized events that can impact the financial performance of a company. A 1996 survey of 240 Fortune 1,000 companies in North America and Europe was commissioned by CenterLine Software, Inc., a company in Cambridge, Massachusetts that developed a software testing tool. The survey found that 12 percent of the companies contacted had faced liability or litigation issues with regard to direct or consequential damages from lack of software quality. With the movement toward e-business and putting software even closer to the customer, we can expect this number to increase in the future. Although process improvement cannot guarantee the elimination of events that could cause bad publicity, improved quality of products and services would reduce the likelihood of such issues.

■ **Processes improve consistency.** Although the heroes of the Information Systems organization may produce high-quality results quickly, the entire organization may have difficulty producing heroic results consistently. Improving processes ensures a consistent level of quality and timeliness of service and support throughout the organization.

■ **Processes increase return on investment.** Jim Stikeleather in *Insane Expectations* (Computerworld Client/Server Journal, November 1995) claims a $5 return for every dollar invested in process improvement. Companies are continually looking into all areas to increase the return on investment. Since many companies still view Information Systems as an expense rather than a competitive asset, they often look at Information Systems to cut expenses and obtain more for each dollar invested. They focus on how to reduce the unit cost of Information Systems. Companies may be willing to spend more money on Information Systems if they are getting a larger return on their investments.

■ **Processes provide the company with a competitive advantage.** Faced with increased competition, companies are asking how they can utilize technology to provide their company with a competitive advantage in the marketplace. Particularly as companies are migrating to e-business, information systems processes must change significantly to handle the increased demands. Increased speed, flexibility, and quality in all processes are becoming an expectation as technology evolves toward e-business.

■ **Processes leverage best practices and solutions.** By establishing and managing proven, repeatable processes, knowledge can be leveraged so that every project gains from previous project experience.

■ **Processes reduce the impact of turnover.** Turnover is high in Information Systems organizations. Employees gain a specific set of knowledge and skills, but that knowledge is in only one person rather than a companywide asset. As employees leave the company, they take their knowledge, skills, and training with them. Best practices and process management turns that expertise into repeatable processes or knowledge that can be used continually within an organization.

■ **Processes improve business productivity and revenue.** As businesses have tightly integrated technology into their business processes, the business can be significantly impacted by the performance of the Information Systems group. If the system is down or a user is waiting for the Help Desk to fix a problem, that user's productivity is impacted. The end customer may also be impacted, as the employee may not be able to properly assist the customer without the system and tools. As a customer, there is nothing more frustrating than calling a company with an order and having the service agent reply that they are unable to assist at that time because the computer is down. In addition to affecting customer satisfaction, it could also impact customer loyalty and market share. Customers unable to wait for technical issues to be resolved will gravitate to another supplier to fill their needs more rapidly.

■ **Processes improve business quality.** Since information is often tightly integrated with how the organization does business with its customers, it is difficult for a company to implement a total quality methodology without including the Information Systems organization. For example, a company may have successfully implemented quality concepts in parts of the organization, but not on a companywide basis. If a customer calls to find the status of an order, the process to provide that information to the customer may be very efficient and effective. However, the customer service representative may provide the customer with inaccurate information because of errors in the systems development process used by Information Systems. In fact, there is often a direct relationship between the quality of systems and the quality of goods and services that a company provides.

■ **Processes prepare for future growth and flexibility.** Without processes in place, as an organization grows there will be a need to increase the number of employees to provide the same level of support. With established processes, productivity is significantly improved and the functions will be organized to handle growth with a minimal increase in employees. Although money may still need to be spent to handle growth, the spending would not be linear.

■ **Processes create a culture of empowered and satisfied employees.** No one enjoys being part of an organization that has a bad reputation or is not meeting expectations. Clear processes and responsibilities enable employees to meet expectations, resulting in increased job satisfaction. The employees will also feel empowered to make changes and resolve issues. With metrics and measures that they can impact, employees aspire for excellence. Information Systems personnel feel valued, understand the expectations, and feel competent to perform their job.

As can be seen in Figure 1.3, the benefits of information systems process improvement outlined above can be realized for the business itself as well as the Information Systems organization.

In fact, many of these benefits are cited as goals when companies begin their process improvement efforts. A research study was done by Gartner Group in 1997 of more than 200 Information Systems departments

Benefits of IS Process Improvement

Business Benefits

- Provides the company with a competitive advantage
- Improves business quality
- Avoids bad publicity
- Strengthens business partnerships
- Improves business revenue
- Increases return on investment
- Prepares for future growth and flexibility
- Improves business productivity
- Improves customer service

IS Benefits

- Improves productivity of IS
- Improves consistency
- Improves effectiveness of project management
- Improves communication
- Leverages best practices and solutions
- Reduces impact of turnover
- Reduces defects, improves quality
- Creates a culture of empowered and satisfied employees
- Improves efficiency

Figure 1.3 Business Benefits of IS Process Improvement

on the benefits of process improvement projects. Figure 1.4 identifies the primary goal reported by these companies beginning process improvement projects.

MARKET DRIVERS

Why is information systems process management important now? What are the market drivers? The META Group (a research company) identified process improvement as a key trend in its 1999 trends for IT Performance Engineering and Measurement Strategies. Specifically, META predicted that in 1999 and 2000, software process improvement and quality programs would continue to stagnate, enabling only micro-level progress on It productivity and quality. However, by 2001 and 2002, they predicted that It will focus on performance engineering as the preferred approach for achieving performance improvements, and by 2002 and 2003, performance engineering approaches will improve productivity and quality to new levels.

There are many forces creating this need for process improvement within Information Systems.

■ **Electronic commerce, e-business, and the Internet.** As companies leverage the use of Intranets and Extranets, there will be an additional need for Information Systems to understand and link

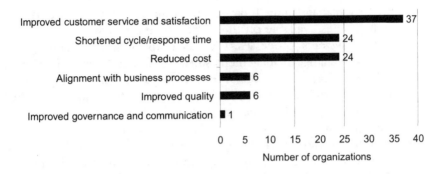

Figure 1.4 Process Improvement Goals

with the processes of other departments within the company. With the advent of e-business and technology our information systems processes are moving closer to and impacting the end customer. In the past, business processes could mask the inadequacies of our information systems processes. For example, if the system was down when a customer called to place an order, the customer service representative could take the information down on paper and call the customer back with a delivery date. Likewise, if the system was not developed properly to fit the business needs, the customer service agent could translate as information was input into the system. With customers placing orders directly into corporate systems, as is done with e-business, any outage in the system or inaccurate design can directly affect the customer. Technology is becoming an integral part of day-to-day business and impacting the success of the business.

■ **Performance demands.** Today, executives are sensitive to total cost of ownership, poor and lengthy application development, and performance issues with systems. Executives are demanding that Information Systems improve their methods and increase overall efficiency and effectiveness of the organization by implementing best practices. There is pressure to do more with less, reduce operating costs, and increase end customer satisfaction. As technology progresses in an organization, users of the technology are becoming more engaged, informed, and demanding. Processes such as Problem Management, Inventory and Asset Management, Change Management, and Understand Requirements are just a few of the processes that may not be well understood or documented within an Information Systems organization.

■ **Changing technology.** The identification and implementation of new information technologies can be an outcome of successful process management. Today, there is an abundance of tools and technologies available on the market to assist in automating information systems processes, such as Help Desk call management software, change management software, and systems management software. These tools can be costly and take time to implement. Many companies have tried to implement the tools and have failed because they applied the technology without understanding and reengineering the process using the technology.

■ **Reliability demands.** Companies today are using technology to provide them with a competitive advantage and market dominance. Growing numbers of companies are implementing technology tightly linked with core business processes. These critical systems must provide guaranteed round-the-clock reliability and scalability (ability to grow with the company to support the business operations). As the core applications become the very livelihood of the business, there is no tolerance for application down time. Internet companies are a prime example of this. Just a few hours of system down time can cause millions of dollars of lost revenue and influence the price of the stock and earnings per share. Fundamental information systems processes such as Availability Management, Capacity Management, Change Control, and Problem Management must be functioning properly to ensure consistent, reliable service and deliver high levels of application availability.

■ **Interdependence.** Business solutions today are dependent on many different pieces that must function together. In the early years, with a mainframe and terminal, troubleshooting was less complex. Today, with client/server solutions, the problem may be on the PC, network, server, main server, database, router, or any number of other areas. As a user, there is nothing more frustrating than being in an organization that reports 99.9 percent availability of their system and yet constantly experiences system down time. To a user, the system is unavailable, whether it is a desktop application or a network issue. Information systems processes and metrics must operate end to end and across organizational boundaries to be effective.

■ **Enterprise Requirements Planning (ERP).** Many companies recently invested significantly in new ERP systems to solve their year 2000 issues. Companies that have experienced the pain and expense of these implementations will be looking at process improvements as a means of finding additional value for their investment.

■ **Outsourcing.** Although the outsourcing movement has made many Information Systems organizations nervous, it is, in fact, an admission by company personnel (usually out of frustration) that they cannot internally produce quality information systems services efficiently and effectively. They turn to outsourcing as a possible answer and catalyst for change to improve the efficiency (or cost, typically) and effectiveness. The outsourcing pronouncements by many organizations are wake-up calls to Information Systems organizations that they must start improving their services or their very survival can be threatened. It is sad to see organizations resort to outsourcing as their only alternative, as information systems can be a competitive advantage if functioning properly. Even if an organization must turn to outsourcing, it is much easier (and less expensive) to outsource a process-based organization.

- **Globalization.** In order to be competitive, companies are finding they must stretch their business across the globe. E-business is also forcing this worldwide movement, because there are no boundaries in cyberspace. Processes must cross over continents and be transparent to the customer, no matter where they are physically in the world.

- **Regulatory requirements.** ISO 9000 audits that focus on defined procedures and processes now include the scope of Information Systems. For many Information Systems organizations, processes and procedures are a new concept, because they may be in a firefighting survival mode. When the internal ISO auditors turn to Information Systems, they often find a tremendous lack of documentation and defined processes.

- **Labor issues.** The short supply of information systems professionals has raised labor costs and requires companies to be more effective in using these costly resources. In the study by Jones, chairman of Software Productivity Research., Inc., in Burlington, Massachusetts, 60 percent of the U.S. software workforce is engaged in fixing errors that would be avoidable if total quality management practices were implemented. If that number is accurate, quality software development processes could lead to a surplus of more than one million personnel, rather than the huge shortage of personnel claimed throughout the industry. In other words, valuable resources are being mismanaged. A process methodology and proper documentation are also methods for companies to sustain through many cycles of information systems staff turnover. Process documentation can also ensure that resources are used efficiently so an expensive technical resource is not doing a function that could be performed by someone else (for example, a database administrator standing in line at the copy machine).

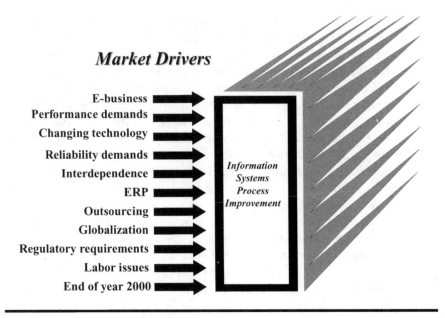

Figure 1.5 Market Drivers

- **End of Year 2000.** With the year 2000 issue resolved, companies will have to begin defining new initiatives that require improved processes. Many companies will also be reducing information systems costs and will need to focus internally to improve their overall efficiency and effectiveness.

As shown in Figure 1.5, there are numerous market drivers encouraging or even dictating improved information systems processes. As global competition increases and technology becomes more critical in business, efficient and effective information systems processes are no longer a competitive advantage, but a fundamental necessity to sustain business and promote growth.

PROCESS EVOLUTION

How do information systems processes evolve? Developing an Information Systems organization to become a world-class organization is an evolution. A culture of continuous improvement must be instilled in the organization. This change, or evolution, does not happen overnight; it takes work, education, and commitment to excellence. For a change to occur, the reward must be greater than the sum of the current pain plus the pain of the change. That is, the organization must truly want to change to begin the process evolution.

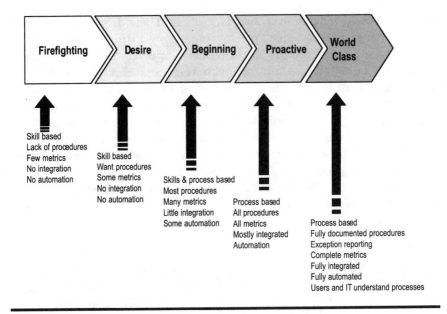

Figure 1.6 Process Evolution

There are five basic stages an organization goes through to evolve into a world-class organization. The stages described in Figure 1.6 are similar to the five levels of maturity that were developed in 1991 with the U.S. Department of Defense by the Software Engineering Institute at Carnegie Mellon University. That model, the Capability Maturity Model for improving the software development process, as well as the model discussed here, maps an evolutionary path from ad hoc, chaotic processes to mature, disciplined, and efficient processes.

Looking at process improvement as a continuum allows companies to take steps toward an improved environment rather than attempt to get there in one move. This breaks the complexity of the process improvement into manageable stages, maps the opportunities for improvement, and recognizes the value of evolution. The stages of process evolution are described in more detail below.

Firefighting

An organization in this stage may be in the firefighting, reactive, or chaotic mode. Each crisis or issue is handled independently, depending upon the skill set of the individual handling the crisis. Success depends on heroes. For example, when one user calls the Help Desk person with an issue, it may get handled totally differently than when another user calls another Help Desk individual with the exact same issue. There are no processes or procedures documented and formalized. There is no commonality across information systems. Projects and support are handled inconsistently. There are few metrics measured and reported. Schedules and cost targets are rarely met, or are met with very unpredictable results. Commitments are made without any process or detail to ensure they can be met. Furthermore, projects are not managed to meet the commitments. In this environment, some individuals may even feel that defined processes stifle creativity and, therefore, process definition is resisted. Another common comment by staff is that they do not have time to implement a more structured approach. Most often this is true, because they are continually in crisis mode. In 1998, the META Group estimated 50 percent of organizations to be in this mode of operation.

Desire

An organization in this stage wants to implement procedures and processes to obtain a more structured approach. Although they are still skills-based, some metrics and procedures may begin to be developed. Some of the individual and heroic efforts may be organized so that they can be repeated. Initial process training may have been conducted, but the concepts are not used extensively. Individuals have heard process concepts and engineering techniques enough to say, "Sure, we do that." Although some project management concepts may be followed, in a crisis, the individuals revert to the firefighting mode of operation. A systems development methodology may have been selected but not fully or consistently implemented. Processes that may receive focus in this stage are those that establish basic information systems controls, such as:

- Schedule Management
- Security Management
- Financial Management
- Vendor Management
- Facilities Management

An estimated 35 percent of Information Systems organizations are in this stage of evolution (META, 1998).

Beginning

In this phase, standard processes are defined, documented, and followed. The organization understands the process, how it works, and what its individual role is in the process. A process management group is established to manage improvements. Process training and communication occurs regularly. This organization may be both process- and skills-based in different areas of the Information Systems organization. Although some areas of the Information Systems organization may have fully implemented process methodology and have documented procedures that are consistently followed, not all areas of the organization may be integrated into the processes. There may be pockets or islands of automation for various steps of a process. There may be many metrics that are measured and reported on a regular basis. Successful processes are repeatable. Reasonable commitments are planned. Schedules, cost, and functionality targets are met on a regular basis. Processes that may receive attention in this phase are those that address both system and organization issues as the organization establishes an infrastructure. These are processes that institutionalize effective practices and management of processes across the function, such as:

- Backup and Disaster Recovery Management
- Problem Management
- Understand Requirements
- Design Solutions
- Construct and Integrate Solutions
- Test Solutions
- Customer Acceptance

An estimated 10 percent of Information Systems organizations is in this stage (META, 1998).

Proactive

In this stage, processes are the natural way. Metrics are collected and used to identify and handle process variation in all areas of the Information Systems organization. Quality targets are established. Targets for cost and time are predictable and reliable. Procedures and processes are well documented and followed with rigor, even in a crunch, in all areas of the Information Systems organization. All individuals in the Information Systems organization have an understanding of all the processes. Processes are integrated across various Information Systems organizations (such as technical support and desktop and business applications). Issues are handled consistently and predictably each time they occur. Automation has been implemented and integrated across all the processes and areas of the organization. Process improvement is a regular part of everyone's job and is reflected as part of job descriptions and performance appraisals. Processes that may receive attention during this phase are those that focus on establishing a quantitative understanding of both the systems and the activities being performed, such as:

- Performance and Availability Management
- Capacity and Storage Management
- Change Management
- Installation and Configuration Management
- Inventory and Asset Management
- Software Distribution Management

Fewer than 5 percent of Information Systems organizations are estimated to be in this stage of development (META, 1998).

World Class

All customer needs are met with quality systems and solutions on a consistent basis. Benchmarking is done regularly to continually improve processes and metrics. The organization is fully process-based, with all procedures and processes well documented and understood. Processes are designed for maximum efficiency and effectiveness. A balanced score-card may have been developed, with metrics posted regularly and all members striving for improvement. Processes are fully integrated and fully automated. Users understand and participate eagerly in the processes. Causes of poor performance are eliminated. New technology and process improvements are prototyped, piloted, and added to the process on a regular basis. Processes that may receive attention in this phase are those that cover the issues related to continual, measurable process improvement, such as:

- Service Level Management
- Information Systems Strategic Planning
- Market Information Systems Offerings
- Customer Satisfaction Management
- Human Resource Management

Fewer than 1 percent of Information Systems organizations are estimated to be in this stage (META, 1998).

BARRIERS TO CHANGE

So, why has it taken so long for Information Systems to embrace process improvement methodologies when they have been practiced for many years within other areas of the business? Why aren't more companies in the world-class category of evolution? Why may some individuals within Information Systems not initially support the improvement efforts? What are the barriers to change from the old way of doing things?

In many areas of the business, processes are repetitive and produce a tangible or deliverable product. Information Systems is about technology and information. It is more of a job-shop environment, as no two projects or problems are really alike. Processes are more difficult to identify, document, and automate in a variable environment. However, when complex problems are broken down into simple steps, commonality can be found.

Information Systems is also a relatively newer discipline than manufacturing and other service areas. There is less structure and organization, and fewer standards have been developed in the information systems industry as a whole compared with other industries. However, there are a growing number of resources available that were not available several years ago. This book is one of those resources.

Typically, Information Systems organizations have a tremendous backlog of requests. In an environment that feels as if one is continually behind, chaotic or firefighting, and continuously pushed to provide more, it is often difficult to take a step back and take the time to improve the tools and processes. Although the job of Information Systems is to improve the tools and processes for others, we are often the last ones to improve our own processes and tools. To get past this barrier, it is critical to step out of the firefighting circular chaos and improve the tools and processes to become more efficient and effective. It is always amazing to see how many Information Systems organizations do not have the time to do a task right, but always have the time to do it over again. If time is spent today preventing tomorrow's problems, less time will need to be spent tomorrow fixing the errors of today!

Some individuals in Information Systems may resist a structured process environment because they claim it will limit their creativity and confine them to a rigid process. Actually, the structured process allows them to more effectively use their creativity in developing solutions for the customer rather than continually fighting the same fires over and over again.

Although it has changed significantly in recent years, in the past, Information Systems was viewed by many organizations as simply an overhead function rather than one adding true value to the business. As an overhead function, budgets were often constrained to the bare minimum. With tight resources, it was difficult to invest resources in improving processes. However, more companies are viewing information systems as a strategic part of the business. Information Systems' budgets continue to climb. Once the initial investment has been made, improved processes will save money.

Many individuals in Information Systems work very hard, but fail to take the viewpoint of their customer. When information systems individuals are asked during an assessment to rate their performance, efficiency, and support, they typically rate themselves relatively high. When the users are also asked to rate the performance of the Information Systems organization, many times their ratings are significantly lower. It is important to realize, when asking a customer or user about the support provided by Information Systems, perception is reality. The Information Systems organization must realize that, although they may be working very hard, the level of service they provide the customer may be totally unacceptable. By focusing on process improvement, IS can establish a common understanding of quality with the customer, measure quality, and celebrate success while moving toward the targets.

Change is always difficult and can be resisted by some individuals. The old ways of doing things become entrenched in the organization, and it may be difficult to see new ways. Chapter 10 outlines in more detail barriers to change and how to help the organization accept change.

How is it possible to get over the barriers to change and move the Information Systems organization through the evolution to become a world-class operation? This book will outline a step-by-step methodology to guide the process improvement effort.

PROCESS IMPROVEMENT TOOLS AND METHODOLOGIES

Process modeling tools can range from simple flowcharting tools to very sophisticated modeling tools with repositories of process models or simulation capability. At the very basic end of the spectrum, sticky notes and flip charts are great tools to use while documenting or designing processes.

Simple flowcharting or drawing tools, such as Visio by Shapeware Corporation, Micrografx's ABC Snapgraphics and ABC Flowcharter, and Process Charter by Scitor Corporation are examples of products that can help. Process mapping software provides more assistance in reengineering, with tools such as BPWin by Logic Works and Plexus by The Jonathon Corporation. There are also process mapping products that support the IDEF (Integrated computer-aided Definition) process mapping methodology, such as AI0 and AI4 by Knowledge Based Systems, Meta Software's Design/IDEF, Texas Instruments' BDF, Wizdom Systems' IDEFine, and AutoSADT by Triune Software. Process simulation software tools, such as Optima by AdvanEdge Technologies, ITHINK by Performance Systems, ProTEM by Software Consultants International, Application Development Consultants ProcessSimulator, and AT&T ISTEL Witness, allow one to analyze the impact of process improvements before implementation. Some of the tools available are shown in Figure 1.7 (although software products and companies change on a continual basis).

Process modeling tools have improved over the past few years in both functionality and ease of use. Most process modeling tools generate

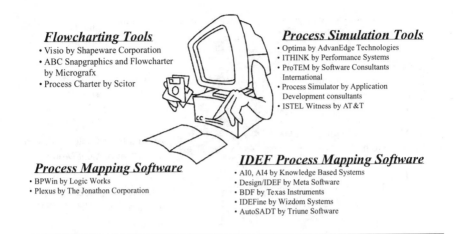

Flowcharting Tools
- Visio by Shapeware Corporation
- ABC Snapgraphics and Flowcharter by Micrografx
- Process Charter by Scitor

Process Simulation Tools
- Optima by AdvanEdge Technologies
- ITHINK by Performance Systems
- ProTEM by Software Consultants International
- Process Simulator by Application Development consultants
- ISTEL Witness by AT&T

Process Mapping Software
- BPWin by Logic Works
- Plexus by The Jonathon Corporation

IDEF Process Mapping Software
- AI0, AI4 by Knowledge Based Systems
- Design/IDEF by Meta Software
- BDF by Texas Instruments
- IDEFine by Wizdom Systems
- AutoSADT by Triune Software

Figure 1.7 Process Tools Examples

workable models, identify tasks within a process, show who performs the tasks, guide task performance, prioritize processes, and outline back-up plans for the process. The tools are typically Internet enabled, allowing browser users to easily view the next steps as well as entire processes. Some tools also provide reference business models of the leading Enterprise Requirements Planning software packages for specific industries, provide a gap analysis between a specific process and the industry process, and do multidimensional analysis. Although it may be helpful, it is not required to have sophisticated and expensive tools before embarking on a process improvement effort. Sometimes it can be helpful to tackle the first few process improvement efforts using more simple tools (such as Visio) to concentrate on the process improvement steps and determine the true requirements of an automated tool.

In addition to charting tools, there are many different methodologies. Methodologies can be intimidating. Some are clear and specific; many are vague and complex. At its core, a methodology guides you down the path of practical improvement with a step-by-step approach. It provides a framework to make decisions, take action, and move forward. Figure 1.8 identifies some of the methodologies associated with information systems processes. This figure shows a variety of methodologies, some are for improving a few specific process areas, while some are general standards or guidelines.

This book is written to present a practical step-by-step methodology, not to explore each of the published methodologies listed. Being aware of these options simply informs one of other existing methodologies that may work in an organization. Many companies spend years developing internal experts and changing their practices

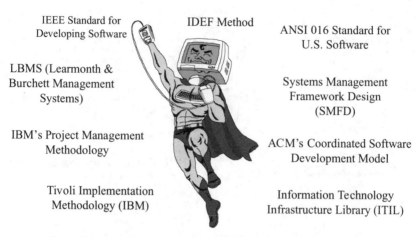

IEEE Standard for
Developing Software

IDEF Method

ANSI 016 Standard for
U.S. Software

LBMS (Learmonth &
Burchett Management
Systems)

Systems Management
Framework Design
(SMFD)

IBM's Project Management
Methodology

ACM's Coordinated Software
Development Model

Tivoli Implementation
Methodology (IBM)

Information Technology
Infrastructure Library (ITIL)

Capability Maturity Model and the IDEAL Methodology (The
Software Engineering Institute at Carnegie Mellon University)

Figure 1.8 Information Systems Process Improvement Methodologies

to align with an improvement methodology. In today's fast paced information systems world, years are not available to implement these changes. The methodology to use is a personal choice. The reason for choosing a methodology is to provide the framework to make decisions, take action, and improve. The methodology is only the means to an end, not the end itself. Do not spend an enormous effort laboring over a particular methodology, rather apply that energy toward the improvements. Whatever is done must be done quickly. Develop an approach, deploy it within the organization, and demonstrate results.

One way to evaluate methodologies is to think about the methodology in terms of approach, deployment, and results, as shown in Figure 1.9.

Figure 1.9 Evaluating Methodologies

Approach

The organization uses a web based ticketing system to manage computer support activities. Requests are submitted via the intranet and uploaded to each technician's palm pilot for remote access in the facility. The system allows for preventive notifications and is tied to routine maintenance schedules. A log of system improvements is kept to demonstrate an ongoing improvement cycle.

Figure 1.10 Approach Example

This model was created through The Malcolm Baldrige Criteria for Performance Excellence and is used to guage the effectiveness of an organization.

Thinking about an improvement methodology in this manner will provide the framework to make decisions, take action, and improve.

- **Approach.** Every methodology represents an approach to improving the operation. In essence it is what you decide to do. For example, using a web-based ticketing system to manage computer support activities is one approach. How effective an approach it may be depends on many factors, such as:
  - Is it unique and innovative?
  - Is it systematic?
  - Is it integrated?
  - Is it prevention based?
  - Does it involve improvement cycles?

Deployment
The organization deploys its online
ticketing system through the intranet
to all departments. Training is
provided during new employee
orientation. Evidence exists showing
the extent of requests by department
for each month as well as the type of
request submitted. Departments with
both high and low activity levels are
reviewed on a monthly basis for
common causes.

Figure 1.11 Deployment Example

> ■ Is it based on quantitative information that is objective and
> reliable?
> The more complete the answers to these questions, the more
> solid the approach and methodology for selecting processes for
> improvements. An example of approach is shown in Figure 1.10.

- **Deployment.** No matter how solid the approach is, without
  effective deployment it is worthless. Deployment refers to the
  extent to which the approach is applied to all relevant areas
  of the organization. In essence it deals with how much is done,
  in both organizational depth and breadth. For example, if "all
  computer users feed ticket requests for all software through
  the web directly to each computer support technician," how
  good the deployment is depends on four encompassing questions:

  - Does the implementation apply to all work units?

Results

The organization can demonstrate a reducing trend of monthly calls that is now 32 percent lower in volume than last year. 73 percent of the ticket requests are communicated and resolved within 12 hours. Follow-up surveys with customers indicate an 86 percent satisfaction level with work. This compares with industry average of 76 percent satisfaction level and the best-in-class benchmark of 95 percent satisfaction.

Figure 1.12 Results Example

- Does the implementation touch all relevant people in each work unit?
- Does the implementation impact all transactions, occurrences, or interactions?
- Does the implementation happen to the full extent?

Again, the more complete the answers are to these questions, the more solid the deployment of the methodology. An example of deployment is shown in Figure 1.11.

■ **Results.** Once an approach is deployed, the next step is to review the results. Results demonstrate the outcome from an approach that was effectively deployed. In essence it deals with how well you did what you set out to do. For example, 73 percent of ticket requests are communicated and resolved within 12 hours. How good the results are depends upon three encompassing questions:

- What is the quality and performance level that is being achieved?

■ Are there sustained improvement trends?
■ Are there comparisons with similar providers and world leaders?

An example of results is shown in Figure 1.12.

KEY POINTS TO REMEMBER

■ With market pressures and changing industry, it is absolutely necessary to continuously improve the efficiency and effectiveness of the information systems processes. Begin improvements now!
■ In addition to the technical aspects of process improvement (e.g., tools, techniques, training, methodologies, and metrics), also consider the behavioral aspects needed (e.g., culture, rewards, organization, responsibilities, values, and beliefs) for the implementation to be successful.
■ Improving processes is an evolution with several stages of maturity. Make progress to move the organization along the continuum toward a world-class organization. Don't strive for perfection, rather strive for improvement.
■ Using a structured methodology and tools when improving processes can improve the odds of success. Many methodologies and tools may meet your needs. Read on or select one and begin efforts today!

NOTES AND IDEAS FOR MY PROCESS IMPROVEMENT EFFORT

2

PROCESS FUNDAMENTALS
OVERVIEW

*"Survival of a species is determined by their ability to adapt to
a changing environment."*

Charles Darwin

PROCESS DEFINITION

What is a process? A process is what we do to produce a product, complete
a task, render a service, or achieve a defined business outcome for a customer.
In other words, it is a defined way of accomplishing an end. A process is
a sequence of activities or logically related tasks or activities that have:

- **Input(s):** Information or material that is required to complete the
  activities necessary to produce the end result
- **Transformation:** The tasks performed to transform or add value
  from the input to the output
- **Output(s):** The specified end result required by the customer or
  another process
- **Supplier:** The person, department, or function that provides the input
- **Customer:** The person, department, or function that receives the output
- **Controls:** Measures and steps to ensure the process is functioning
  properly
- **Feedback:** Customer-provided input as to the efficiency and effec-
  tiveness of the process
- **Owner:** The individual who owns the process and is responsible
  for the process efficiency and effectiveness from end to end

27

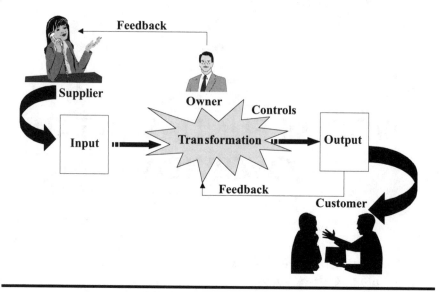

Figure 2.1 Process Components

These process components are depicted in Figure 2.1.

A process can be analyzed as well as grouped with similar processes. Processes can be grouped into an Area, a set of processes that relate to a similar area and function. Processes are a set of activities that focus on one action. Processes can be decomposed into Activities, sets of detailed steps necessary to deliver the end result. Activities can be further broken down into Steps, tasks needed to be done to deliver the end result. This is depicted in Figure 2.2.

Recognize, from the example provided in Figure 2.2, the different levels of detail for each of the groupings. It is important that the team talks about on the same level of detail when discussing the processes.

PROCESS STAKEHOLDERS

Who is involved in a process? Throughout the various levels of a process, there are usually at least four types of process stakeholders, people who have a relationship and vested interest in the performance of the process. Some complex processes may have even more stakeholders. As shown in Figure 2.3, the process stakeholders include:

■ **Customers:** Customers are the recipients or users of the products and services produced in the process. This could be someone in Finance who uses a PC and network established by Information Systems. This person may call the Help Desk for support

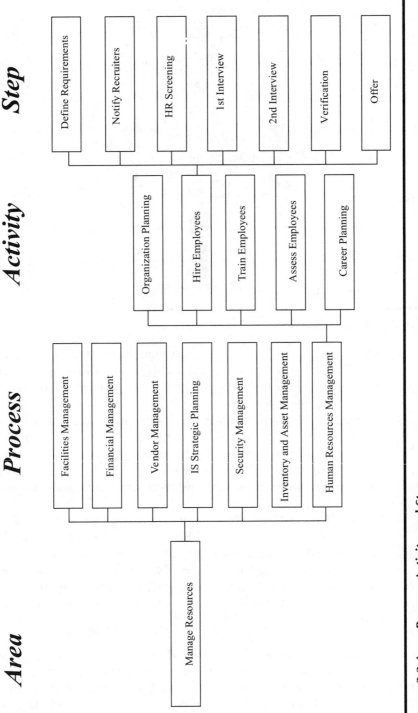

Figure 2.2 Area, Process, Activity, and Step

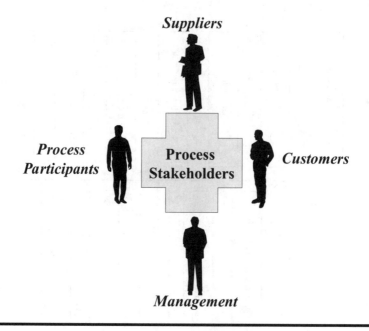

Figure 2.3 Process Stakeholders

issues and receive assistance. Customer satisfaction can be measured by user surveys. For many information systems processes, the customers are typically internal business users of the information systems services.

■ **Suppliers:** Suppliers provide input into the process. For example, if IBM provided systems maintenance on server hardware, IBM would be a supplier that could impact the availability process. For many information systems processes, the suppliers are typically internal business users of the information systems services.

■ **Process Participants:** These are individuals who actually perform the process. For example, the Help Desk individuals would be involved in the problem management process.

■ **Management:** Management may establish policies and procedures, standards, and metrics. It may also provide or fund resources used in the process. Management is often responsible for the functioning of the process.

Each of these stakeholders may have a different interest in the process, may define the success of the process differently, and may benefit from the process performance in different ways. When redesigning a given process, it is important to consider the desires of all the stakeholders of

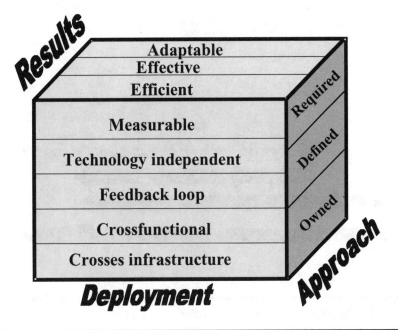

Figure 2.4 Characteristics of a Good Process

the process and to satisfy and balance the diverse interests of all the various process stakeholders.

PROCESS CHARACTERISTICS

Figure 2.4 depicts the characteristics for the approach, deployment, and results of a successful information systems process. A detailed description of these features and qualities is provided below.

- **Required:** The process is required to support a key business function. The objectives of the process are related to the mission and objectives of Information Systems and the business. Processes are reevaluated over time to ensure that they are still required.
- **Defined:** The process has a specific beginning and end with a specific scope and deliverables. It is fully documented and the documentation is up to date.
- **Owned:** Each process has an owner responsible for improving the process. The process owner establishes procedures and guidelines, develops measurements and reports, ensures quality, implements process improvements, and interfaces with other process owners.

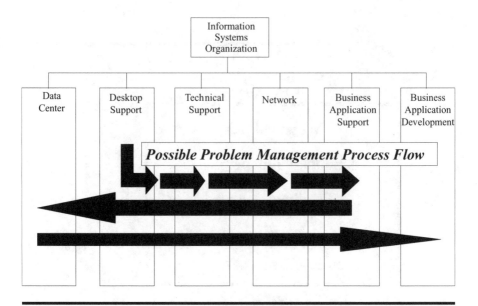

Figure 2.5 Processes Crossing Organization Structure

The process owner has sufficient resources and authority to attain process objectives.

■ **Measurable:** Results are quantifiable. Attainment of process objectives is measured and monitored on a regular basis.

■ **Technology independent:** Changing technology does not significantly impact the functioning of the process. New technology can be added as necessary.

■ **Feedback loop:** The process alerts the process owner or participants to the efficiency and effectiveness of the process.

■ **Cross-functional:** Processes should not be constrained by the organizational structure. Rather, as shown in Figure 2.5, processes flow across the organizational structure. For example, a problem may be entered in the Desktop Support organization. If the Desktop organization is unable to solve the issue, the problem may be passed off to the Technical Support Group. The Technical Support Group may determine that it is a network issue. After further investigation, the Network Group may determine that the problem is actually an application issue. The Application Support Group determines that to solve the issue, an application program may need to be developed. This is just one example of a single issue causing a process to span across traditional silos in the Information Systems organization itself.

■ **Crosses infrastructure:** Processes work across the different layers of infrastructure, regardless of the technology or layer of

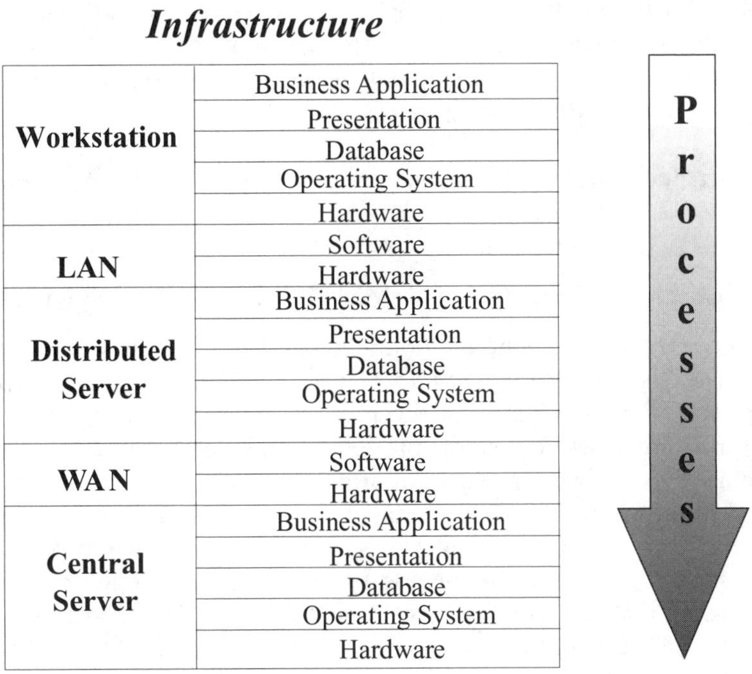

Infrastructure

Workstation	Business Application
	Presentation
	Database
	Operating System
	Hardware
LAN	Software
	Hardware
Distributed Server	Business Application
	Presentation
	Database
	Operating System
	Hardware
WAN	Software
	Hardware
Central Server	Business Application
	Presentation
	Database
	Operating System
	Hardware

Processes

Figure 2.6 Processes Cross Infrastructure Components

infrastructure. This is shown in Figure 2.6. For example, a normal operating systems upgrade on a PC environment may cause some databases to be modified. The upgrade may necessitate an update in the LAN software (e.g., a new release of Novell may be needed to be compatible with a new release of Windows), which may also lead to some modifications in the distributed or central server or wide area network. This is just one example where a process may cross through and impact various layers of technology.

■ **Efficient:** The process optimizes the resources (human and capital) that are used and is automated with the use of tools for maximum efficiency. Personnel requirements have been reduced because of the efficiency of the process. The process has been assessed and improved and unnecessary steps and interventions have been eliminated. Measurements are reviewed and improved on a regular basis.

■ **Effective:** The process achieves the desired results. User (those who receive output from the process) satisfaction is measured regularly. The process is defined, thoroughly documented, and understood by all participants.

- ■ **Adaptable:** The process maintains effectiveness and efficiency as the business requirements change and adapts to a change in personnel or technology. Such changes do not significantly impact the functioning of the process.

A detailed checklist for these process characteristics is outlined in Appendix A.

PROCESS IMPROVEMENT METHODOLOGY OVERVIEW

The process improvement methodology outlined in this book contains seven basic steps, as depicted in Figure 2.7. The first three steps are completed at the beginning of the process improvement effort. In order to improve information systems processes significantly, the effort must be recognized as a formal project. An attempt to just improve processes as time permits will not result in significant progress. The effort will probably not receive the attention, resources, and commitment that it requires to successfully implement the necessary changes. By recognizing process improvement as a formal project, one can identify the project team, determine a plan, obtain the resources and commitment necessary to complete the effort, establish the priority relative to other projects, and obtain support for the effort. The second step identifies all the processes within the information systems environment, while the third step prioritizes and selects the processes to improve.

Steps four through seven are completed for each process requiring improvement. In step four, the current process is outlined and analyzed. In step five, a plan to improve the process is developed. In step six, a new and improved process is designed. Finally, in step seven, the new process is implemented.

The seven steps described above are outlined in detail in each of the subsequent chapters of this book. An overview of the seven basic steps is provided below:

Getting Started

As will be discussed in Chapter 3, the first step outlines the tasks to start the process improvement effort and reviews the information systems strategic plan, the business and operational plans, and the documentation. The goals and objectives for the process improvement effort must be grounded in the business and information systems plans and direction. If an information systems plan has not been developed, the strategic planning process must begin.

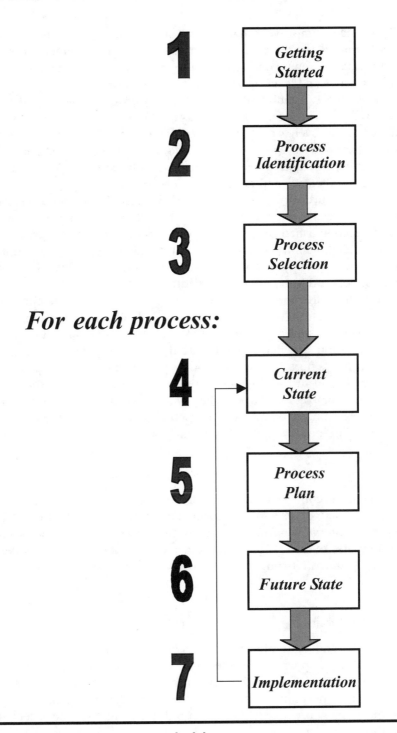

Figure 2.7 Process Improvement Methodology

One can't improve what is not understood. Time must be spent understanding the current information systems environment, reviewing documentation, and conducting interviews in order to understand the current issues and level of pain in the organization.

Once this is established, the process improvement goals and metrics are developed. These metrics will measure the progress of the improvement effort and the overall effectiveness and efficiency of Information Systems. The metrics chosen will be based on the business and information systems plans. An information systems scorecard should be developed to measure the overall efficiency and identify key objectives.

With improvement goals formulated, the Case for Action to justify and communicate the improvement effort is built, and the goals — or what can be accomplished by improving the information systems processes — are identified. Identifying the goals and building the Case for Action will help garner the support and enthusiasm of both the Information Systems organization and business management.

With the direction established, a steering team to guide the process improvement effort is formed; the roles and responsibilities, logistics of team meetings, and any tools that will be used for communication and documentation are determined; and the project plan for the process improvement effort is developed. This plan includes the detailed tasks, time frame, and responsibilities of those involved as well as the methodology (deliverables) and tools that will be used for the effort. Finally, before beginning to work on process improvement, the project team is trained in the process methodology and tools.

Process Identification

During the second step, which will be discussed in Chapter 4, all the processes that exist within Information Systems are identified. This is begun by interviewing to understand the current activities, tasks, inputs, and outputs. As the current processes are identified, the process description is documented and benefits and issues with the current process are noted.

Process Selection

The impact and value of each process are analyzed during the third step, discussed in Chapter 5. Processes will be prioritized to determine which to work on first. Several different approaches, including criteria-based, consensus, opportunity, metrics, and the evolution approach, are outlined for prioritizing processes. The top processes will then be selected for improvement or reengineering.

Current State Process Assessment

During the fourth step, which is discussed in Chapter 6, additional information will be gathered to improve the process. Information can be gathered by conducting interviews, observing the process, or performing the process. Next, the current process is flowcharted using a Cross-Functional Flowchart. Time is added to the flowchart and a Value Added Ratio calculated to measure the efficiency of the process. The current process is then analyzed for improvement.

Process Plan

During the fifth step, outlined in Chapter 7, the objectives and vision for the new process are determined. The process metrics will be identified to measure the efficiency and effectiveness of the process; baseline data will be studied to understand how the process is presently performing; the process will be benchmarked against other processes in the industry; and finally, the project plan to improve the process is developed. This plan includes forming the project team to improve the process, developing the Case for Action which outlines why the process should be improved, and identifying the specific tasks and deliverables for the process improvement effort.

Future State Process Mapping

During the sixth step, discussed in Chapter 8, the new process will be designed, developed, and documented. Organizing the redesign sessions is begun by consolidating the process knowledge and gathering the right people. A process owner will be identified and his or her roles and responsibilities documented. The new process will be built through redesign sessions with a sharp focus on the process objectives. Various design techniques as well as suggested best practices will be presented. The final result will be a new cross-functional flowchart of the new and improved flow. The new process will be validated by reviewing the objectives and elements of the process. A risk analysis will be performed to further understand the impact of the new process. Finally, the supporting process documentation necessary to communicate and implement the new process will be developed.

Implementation

In the seventh step, the impact on people and technology is determined and the implementation plan for the new process established. Risk management will also be a part of the implementation plan. The new process will then be implemented, which may include changes in technology, people/organization, and procedures. Finally, the new process is continuously monitored and improved.

Remember that steps four through seven will be repeated for each process that is selected for improvement. The time frame for each step will depend on many factors, such as:

- Size of organization
- Level of involvement and commitment to the process project
- Amount of change involved
- Technology impacted
- Organizational impact
- Complexity of environment

The process should move quickly. A quick pace should be established or the process improvement project will last forever. It is important to get through this first process improvement project rather quickly to establish momentum. So, let's learn more about each of these steps.

KEY POINTS TO REMEMBER

- Processes typically cross organization structures and technology components. Design the process to smoothly and consistently flow across these entities.
- Ask if the process is still required.
- Processes should have metrics reported regularly to measure the effectiveness and efficiency of the process.
- A single individual should own a process from end to end.
- Consider input from all the various process stakeholders before modifying a process. This includes suppliers, customers, management, and process participants.
- The process improvement methodology presented in this book has seven basic steps: Getting Started, Process Identification, Process Selection, Current State Process Assessment, Process Plan, Future State Process Mapping, and Implementation.
- Keep the project moving at a quick pace.

NOTES AND IDEAS FOR MY PROCESS IMPROVEMENT EFFORT

3

GETTING STARTED

"The longest march starts with the first step."

Mao Tse-Tung, *Thoughts of Chairman Mao*

So, we are ready to start our journey on process improvement. Congratulations! Recognizing the need and getting started are major accomplishments. Where do we go from here?

PLANNING

As outlined in the overview of the process improvement methodology, the first step is Getting Started. It is here where the process improvement project is planned. In this step, the following tasks will be completed:

- **Information Systems Strategic Plan:** Review the information systems strategic plan. If one has not been developed, begin a strategic planning effort.
- **Project Goals:** Review or develop process and project goals and information systems metrics to measure progress. Identify what will be accomplished by improving information systems processes; build the Case for Action.
  - Information Systems Metric
  - Customer Satisfaction Metric
  - Information Systems Balanced Scorecard
  - Metrics Evolution
  - Process Improvement Goals

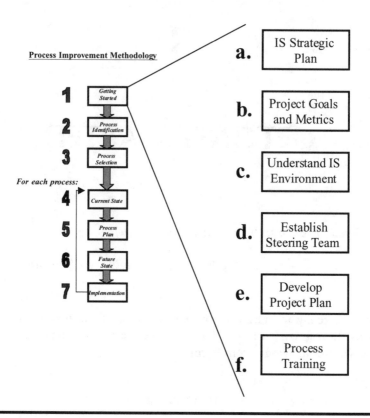

Figure 3.1 Getting Started Tasks

- **Understand the IS Environment:** Understand the current information systems environment through documentation and interviews. Understand the current issues.
- **Establish the Steering Team:** Establish the process improvement steering team and document roles and responsibilities. Determine the logistics of team meetings and tools that will be used for communication and documentation.
- **Develop the Project Plan:** Develop a project plan that outlines the detailed tasks, time frame, and responsibilities.
  - Case for Action
  - Contents of Plan
- **Process Training:** Train the project team in process methodology.

The steps for this first phase, Getting Started, are depicted in Figure 3.1. Following, each task is discussed in more detail.

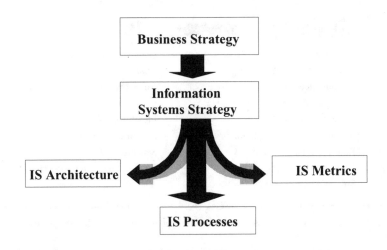

Figure 3.2 Business Strategy Driver

INFORMATION SYSTEMS STRATEGIC PLAN

Having an information systems strategic plan in place is a basic requirement for a world-class Information Systems organization. It is also important for the success of the business. Based on research done by CogniTech, the degree or effectiveness of alignment of Information Systems with the business is important. After measuring 150 enterprises, those that had the highest scores for effectiveness of alignment were also above average in profitability in their industry. Conversely, the lower the effectiveness of alignment scores, the more likely the enterprise had below-average profitability.

An information systems strategic plan is also critical as a foundation for a process improvement effort, because it establishes the framework, priorities, focus, and metrics for process improvement. Knowing what we want to become or where we want to be is essential before beginning a reengineering effort. The strategic plan is an ongoing process that is updated by the business on a regular basis as the business plans change. In a previous book, *A Practical Guide to Information Systems Strategic Planning*, author Anita Cassidy outlines the importance of information systems strategic planning and provides a step-by-step planning approach based on the business direction.

As depicted in Figure 3.2, the business strategy drives the information systems strategy through the strategic planning process. The information systems strategy then defines the technical architecture, information systems process, and resulting metrics that are important.

For example, if a company has a stated business strategy to be a low-cost producer, this would drive the information systems strategy and the resulting architecture to be a provider of low cost, efficient technology (see

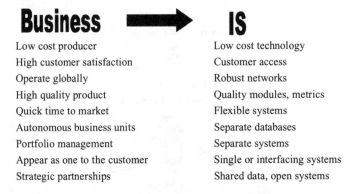

Business	IS
Low cost producer	Low cost technology
High customer satisfaction	Customer access
Operate globally	Robust networks
High quality product	Quality modules, metrics
Quick time to market	Flexible systems
Autonomous business units	Separate databases
Portfolio management	Separate systems
Appear as one to the customer	Single or interfacing systems
Strategic partnerships	Shared data, open systems

Figure 3.3 Different Business Strategies Require Different IS Strategies

Figure 3.3). The information systems environment in this company would be very cost conscious, with return on investment closely scrutinized on all projects. The financial management process would be a key process, with financial metrics receiving much attention.

Contrast that environment with another company that has high customer satisfaction as the stated business objective. Providing customer access to systems and information would be a critical driver of this information systems environment, with focus on electronic commerce, web access, etc. as a foundation for their architecture. Metrics that would be critical in this environment would be service level agreement achievement and problem or call resolution to ensure maximum system availability. Processes that should receive attention would be problem, change, and customer satisfaction management.

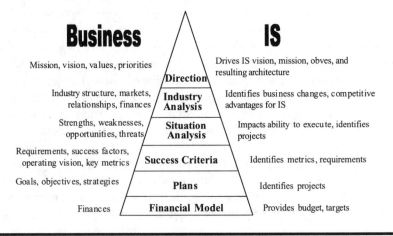

Figure 3.4 Business Plan Driving the IS Plan

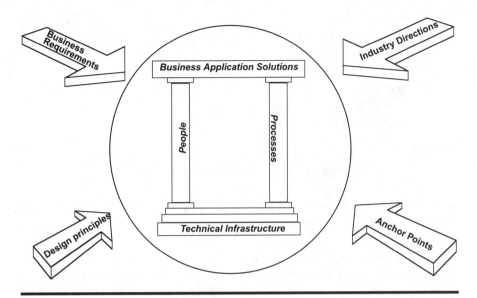

Figure 3.5 Architecture Components

Another company has the business objective of having highly innovative and state-of-the-art products. They value quick time-to-market for their product development cycle. The key information systems strategy in this environment would be to have flexible systems that could meet the changing product needs quickly. Key information systems processes would be in the business applications areas and in constructing and integrating solutions. Key metrics would be the percentage of projects delivered on time and median time to market for systems and changes.

As depicted in Figure 3.4, each component of the business plan in some way drives a component in the information systems plan, processes, and metrics.

The information systems plan contains the direction or architecture not only for the business applications, but also for the people/organization, processes, and technical infrastructure (see Figure 3.5). All of these components are impacted by the business requirements, design principles, industry directions, and anchor points (current investments that cannot be changed quickly or easily).

The architecture for business applications, technical infrastructure, people, and processes is developed by considering the assumptions or anchor points and the drivers or reasons for the change. Finally, the logical and physical design can be determined. This is shown in Figure 3.6. Many companies actually start with the logical and physical design (e.g., should we be Novell or NT, UNIX or AS/400, software packages or custom built?).

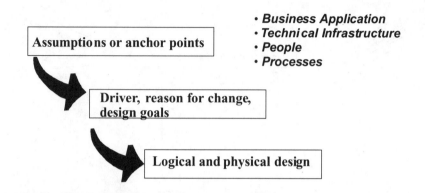

Figure 3.6 Architecture Development

Before beginning a process improvement effort, the business plan and the information systems strategic plan are reviewed. Consider updating the business plan if it does not have the following components:

- Business goals tied to the business mission
- Major business opportunities identified
- Business threats identified and prepared for
- Customers and value chain defined
- Competition tracked
- Strengths and weaknesses of the business identified objectively
- A sensible business strategy established
- A believable forecast in place
- An organization ready for change and the ability to implement the plan
- A clear, concise, and up-to-date business plan
- The entire management team on-board and supporting the plan

Consider updating the plan if the information systems strategic plan does not have the following components or criteria:

- A documented, up-to-date information systems strategic plan
- Business management (executive and production) involved in the development, approval, and maintenance of the plan
- Business objectives and strategies identified
- Business case justification
- High-level information systems direction (e.g., vision, mission, objectives, architecture)
- Architecture identified for business applications, people/organization, processes, and technical infrastructure.
- Projects tied to high-level objectives and business objectives

Business	**_IS_**

■ Current business situation
  ■ Business description
  ■ Business strengths, weaknesses
  ■ Business opportunities, threats
  ■ Industry analysis
 	
■ Business direction
 	
  ■ Business plan: vision, mission, values
  ■ Business success criteria
  ■ Business operating vision
  ■ Business value chain
  ■ Business goals, objectives, strategies
  ■ Business balanced scorecard
  ■ Business processes
  ■ Business requirements
  ■ Information needs
	■ IS current situation
	  ■ IS description (business application, technical infrastructure, people, IS processes)
	  ■ IS strengths, weaknesses
	  ■ IS opportunities, threats
	  ■ Industry information, best practices
	■ IS direction and recommendations
	  ■ IS balanced scorecard
	  ■ Business application
	  ■ E-business (strategic direction, physical architecture, network design, logical architecture, operations issues, future expansion)
	  ■ Data architecture
	  ■ Technical infrastructure
	  ■ IS people/organization
	  ■ IS processes
	  ■ Roadmap

Exhibit 3.1 Information Systems Strategic Plan Aligned with Business Plan

- ■ Information systems opportunities identified
- ■ Information systems threats identified
- ■ Competitors' information systems situation understood
- ■ Information systems projects identified for business applications, people/organization, processes, and technical infrastructure as well as prioritized and scheduled
- ■ The budget tied to the projects and obtainable
- ■ The management team (information systems and business) on board and supportive of the direction and changes

When an information systems strategic plan is in place, before beginning the process improvement effort, the plan should be reviewed to understand what is important to the organization and where it is going.

From this, information systems processes and metrics which will be most important to the organization should be identified. Exhibit 3.1 identifies some of the key components for developing an information systems plan that is aligned with the business plan.

PROJECT GOALS

Now that the direction of the business and Information Systems has been reviewed, proper metrics or measures must support this direction. These metrics also determine the goals for the overall process improvement effort.

Metrics

Utilizing metrics in the goal-setting step is critical to a successful Information Systems organization. As the saying goes, "You can't improve what you can't measure." Metrics challenge us to improve and progress. Metrics provide a standard to measure against, either external (world-class) or internal (historical). Metrics are measures of the vital signs of an Information Systems organization. They tell the organization how healthy it is, how well it performs a process, and how well it achieves specific goals. A study looking at 40 major companies done by the Concours Group revealed that the Information Systems departments with performance measurements did better and had more support from senior management than those that did not. Effectively measuring performance can lead to improved performance. Metrics communicate the performance of Information Systems to business management in a clear, concise, and reliable manner and highlight what is important to the organization. Metrics demonstrate to business management that the Information Systems function is being managed and measured. Metrics allow both the business and Information Systems organization to see performance trends and improvements. Metrics should be viewed as navigational data rather than as conclusions or destinations.

Metrics are the foundation of a continuous improvement process. They allow improvements to be made on the basis of facts and data rather than hunches or opinions. The metric is the indicator; the process is what must be improved. Typically, metrics are concerned with delivering information systems services and products at the lowest cost, with the highest quality, and in the shortest amount of time to optimize value and service. Tracking and measuring metrics is an on-going journey, not a singular event. Simply implementing metrics will not guarantee success or improvements. This implementation must reflect an entire change in management philosophy. Metrics are only as good as the leadership behind them.

Exhibit 3.2 shows a sample of various information systems metrics used at various companies. Although the metrics in the exhibit are presented by functional area, these metrics could also be separated into categories by goals:

- Productivity
- Quality
- Delivery
- Asset Management
- Human Resources

or by areas of efficiency and effectiveness:

- Is Information Systems doing the right things?
- Is it doing them well?
- Is Information Systems assisting the business with the strategic direction?

or in the area of management perspective:

- Strategic metrics
- Tactical metrics
- Operational metrics

or by the various stakeholders or positions of interest:

- Employees
- Internal Operations
- Financial
- Innovation and Learning
- Customer Value
- Business Value

Metrics and categories for measurement should be chosen to fit the environment, goals, and objectives.

Metrics that support the information systems guiding principles are used to measure the success of the Information Systems organization relative to the identified goals. However, be careful about which metrics are selected to track and measure. It is critical that metrics properly reflect and are in alignment with the business and information systems strategies. Metrics reflect how the company goes to market, delivers value, or obtains a competitive edge, whether it is innovation, speed, quality, service, or cost. Metrics must be consistent with the information systems mission, values,

Overall IS

- IS expenditures as a percent of revenue
- IS expenditures per employee
- Revenue per IS dollar
- Total IS expense budget versus actual (and by area within IS)
- Total IS capital budget versus actual
- Employees supported per IS employee
- User satisfaction survey results
- IS employee satisfaction survey results
- IS turnover (by reason)
- Average tenure
- Training hours per IS employee and by skill level
- Overtime per month by skill level
- Percent of employees in support, management, maintenance, and development roles
- Span of control
- Percent of contractors to employees
- Number of open positions
- Average time positions are open
- Number of telecommuters
- Number of internal promotions
- User service level agreements
- Hardware, software, services, staff, overhead, supplies as a percent of total IS budget
- Percent IS budget increase/decrease
- Percent of areas using formal methods and processes
- Rework cost: internal cost of rework across all IS processes

Applications

- Percent of IS spending on legacy systems (keeping the business functioning), including cost by system
- Percent of spending on top business priorities (moving the business forward)
- Sales revenue generated by IS initiatives
- Return on investment by project
- IS yield: ratio of projected value of IS projects to actual benefits attained
- Cost of quality: cost of cancelled projects and system failures
- Percent of applications under service level agreements
- Percent of service level compliance
- Call volume or problems reported by application and root cause
- Percent of applications that are custom compared with package software
- Number of modifications to package software
- Percent of software applications on current release
- Cost per function point
- On-time completion rate of function point
- Percent development/support costs
- Backlog in month and number of requests
- Percent projects on time, on budget, met user requirements

Exhibit 3.2 Information Systems Metrics

Help Desk

- Total cost of ownership of PC
- Amount of time between requesting and obtaining PC
- Cost per call to Help Desk
- Ratio of PCs per employee
- Ratio of PCs per Help Desk employee
- Number of calls per PC
- Number of calls per Help Desk employee
- Number of calls resolved by time slice
- Number of calls by user group
- Help Desk calls by type
- Percent calls resolved on first call
- Average time calls open
- Abandoned call rate
- User satisfaction survey statistics
- Time caller on hold or until answered

Network

- Cost per device or local area network (LAN) port
- Percent utilization by line segment
- Network availability percent
- Network response time
- Mean time to repair
- LAN ports supported by LAN administrator
- LAN hardware, management cost per LAN port
- Mean time to get project, modification implemented

- Percent of user participation by project
- Percent of requests serviced by users
- Number of user stored queries
- Number of users requesting access to tools
- Number of user requested changes, projects
- Number of incident reports
- Number of changes to design
- User satisfaction survey of applications
- Percent of time spent on testing
- Number of errors or defects per module
- Number of lines of code reused
- Backlog cost: the total dollar value of all work waiting to be completed
- Backlog aging: the projected dollar value of work beyond 30, 60, and 90 days of original planned start date

Data Center

- Costs per MIPS or combined power rating
- Cost of service per user
- Percent system availability
- Percent utilization per server
- Average response time
- Memory, disk utilization statistics
- Installed release level of software compared with industry available release
- Turnaround time for key batch jobs
- Total on-time delivery percentage

Exhibit 3.2 continued

Business Strategy	IS Strategy	IS Metric
Low cost producer	Low cost technology	IS expenses as a percent of revenue
High customer satisfaction	Customer access	Customer satisfaction survey
Operate globally	Robust networks	Worldwide average response time
High quality product	Quality modules, metrics	Number of incident reports
Quick time to market	Flexible systems	Mean to implement change

Figure 3.7 Different Business Strategies Require Different IS Strategies and Metrics

objectives, and strategic direction. What does the company expect from information systems? Is it to generate revenue (improve time to market, improve customer service, open new distribution channels), transform the business (streamline operations, provide business information), or reduce costs? Metrics for each strategy would be different, as shown in Figure 3.7.

One set of metrics does not fit all companies. What a company measures strongly affects the behavior of employees. As another saying goes, "Be careful what you measure; you may get it." For a company striving to be a technological leader in their market, tracking and driving down IS costs may not be the most important measure, because running lean may restrict the ability to expand, enable, or enhance business growth or strategic opportunities. Perhaps a more critical measure for this company would be the time to get new projects or modifications implemented, as the speed may impact their technological leadership.

Do not track too many metrics. Five to six key metrics should be selected for the company and kept simple and understandable. The metrics should be communicated regularly, and reward mechanisms should be linked to achievements in these areas. The information systems team must understand, believe, and feel passionate about the metrics for the metrics to be effective.

Care should be taken when comparing metrics to those in the industry or other companies, as analysis can be complex. When comparing to the industry, one must ensure that consistent components are being used. As a metric is decomposed, it is possible to find hidden issues that get masked at a higher level. A metric should be reviewed in perspective with other metrics as this may tell a different story than one stand-alone metric may reveal. Be careful not to drive a metric too far. For example, the organization may be so lean that it actually hampers delivery of robust services, because the organization is driven to a reactive mode rather than a proactive mode. There are trade-off's that need to be considered among metrics and technology, labor, and service level. Driving down information systems costs may simply shift the costs to the user areas where they become hidden and unmanageable costs.

Metrics should be instituted that measure both the efficiency and effectiveness of Information Systems. Effectiveness measures are difficult to identify as they measure what value information systems are bringing to the business. Many times, too much focus is placed on cost reduction rather than finding ways to generate increased value or revenues. One example of an effectiveness measure is user (or internal customer) satisfaction survey results.

The metrics should be collected using consistent methods. Management must be committed to the measurement process in terms of adequate staffing and funding. Metrics should be used and collected as part of the process by the people within the process. Once all the metrics are in place, targets must be set and improvements tracked toward the targets. Celebrate success!

Customer Satisfaction Metric

One of the key metrics for measuring how Information Systems is doing overall as an organization is to ask the internal customers, regularly obtaining input and feedback from customers through a process. Some ways in which Information Systems can obtain this valuable feedback include:

■ Annual customer surveys
■ Surveys that are automatically sent when service requests or problem reports are closed
■ Project post-mortem surveys and reviews

Appendix B shows one example of an annual customer survey.

If an annual customer survey will be conducted, following are suggestions:

■ Keep the survey short, simple, specific, and understandable. State questions in nontechnical language. The customers will not want to take a significant amount of time to complete the survey. Yet, for the results to be meaningful, they need to be specific enough for the survey evaluators to be able to draw accurate conclusions.
■ In addition to areas for comments, try to have as many ratings as possible that are measurable. The comments provide valuable insight into the issues, but the metrics are useful for providing summary information and year-to-year comparisons.
■ Be sure to provide feedback of the survey results to the customers.

IS has formal service-level agreements with customer	1 2 3 4 5
IS conducts formal customer satisfaction surveys on a regular basis	1 2 3 4 5
Informal feedback from customer	1 2 3 4 5
Regular communication to the user community	1 2 3 4 5
Relative comparison of cost-efficiency of specific IS services	1 2 3 4 5
Comparison of overall IS spending with other organizations in our industry	1 2 3 4 5
Ability to reduce or contain IS costs	1 2 3 4 5
Contribution to financial performance of the company	1 2 3 4 5
Contribution of IS to the business goals, strategies, and direction	1 2 3 4 5
Speed and timeliness of applications development process	1 2 3 4 5
Quality of application development	1 2 3 4 5
Availability and reliability of the systems	1 2 3 4 5
Speed and timeliness of support	1 2 3 4 5

Exhibit 3.3 Information System Performance Rating

- If a survey is conducted, plan to take action! It can be frustrating to a customer to give feedback about what is wrong and see no improvements.
- Obtain input on the survey before sending it out. Once the survey comes back, you may think of additional questions and issues that you wished you would have inquired about. Having more individuals who have input into the design of the survey will improve the likelihood that all the issues are considered in advance.
- Consider analysis of the results while designing the survey.
- Make sure the media is appropriate to the audience. Do not prepare a sophisticated online Intranet survey application if most of the customers do not have access or the inclination to use the online system. On the other hand, do not add paper to a paperless environment. Consider what works best in the culture.
- Ask some identification questions, such as the department where the customer is located. Results may vary significantly by area of the organization and this may be very helpful when analyzing the results.

Information Systems Assessment

Business User Perspective:	Score
1. The current systems and tools meet the needs of the business.	3
2. The users have access to the information they need.	2
3. The training and documentation on the systems meets the user needs.	2
4. The systems are available and stable.	4
5. The users know who to contact in IS when they have an issue.	4
6. The users can get critical problems resolved quickly.	3
7. The users can get solutions to business problems in a timely manner.	3
8. The quality of the IS solutions and tools meets the needs.	3
9. Projects are delivered on time, on budget, with promised results.	3
10. IS personnel understand the business and business needs.	3
11. IS has a good strategic direction aligned with the business direction.	2
12. The users know what IS is working on and what tools are available and are notified in advance of changes.	2
13. The users are able to provide input into IS direction and systems.	2
14. IS provides a strategic advantage to the business.	2
15. Overall assessment of IS.	3

Processes:

1. IS has good, documented processes, policies, and procedures that are consistently followed.	1
2. Metrics and measures are used and reported on a regular basis.	1
3. IS has formal service level agreements with users.	1
4. IS conducts formal customer satisfaction surveys on a regular basis.	2
5. IS seeks and listens to informal feedback from users.	2

Systems and Infrastructure:

6. Proper security measures have been taken.	2
7. Hardware and software have been standardized.	4
8. Minimal customization has been made to software.	4
9. IS services are provided on a cost-efficient basis.	3
10. IS has the budget and money necessary to do the job.	3

Information Systems Organization:

11. Roles and responsibilities are clearly defined for IS personnel.	2
12. IS personnel are satisfied, encouraged, and rewarded to do their best.	2
13. There is a lot of teamwork within IS, with a positive can-do attitude.	1
14. Individuals are given the opportunity to make decisions and grow.	3
15. IS has the necessary people resources, staff, and training to do the job.	1
16. Leadership is effective.	3

Exhibit 3.4 Information Systems Assessment

As the survey is designed, think of how the results will be segregated so that they will be most meaningful.

■ Encourage honest feedback, and explain that the information will be used to identify ways to improve the information systems environment. Follow up on specific issues of the survey, but never attack an individual for identifying issues, even if you do not agree with them. Remember that perception is reality. Customer focus groups can also be an effective means of obtaining additional information and feedback.

■ It is helpful to run a test of the survey and tally results to be sure it will give the information desired. For example, the Information Systems group could complete the survey on a trial basis while also providing input into the survey format.

It is important to assess your own information systems performance. Exhibit 3.3 shows one company's rating criteria.

Exhibit 3.4 shows another example of how one IS organization assessed its overall performance. The first section was summarized from customer surveys, while the internal sections were assessed by Information Systems itself.

Information Systems Balanced Scorecard

Many companies have implemented a balanced scorecard very successfully on the business side to obtain improved profitability, sales, and quality as well as other improvements. The balanced scorecard dates back to a 1990 study by The Nolan Norton Institute that documented the feasibility and benefits of implementing a balanced measurement system around four areas — financial, customer, internal processes, and innovation and learning of the people. The balanced scorecard recognizes that no single measure can provide a clear picture of how an organization is functioning; this requires a set of key indicators. This method allows one to focus on what is really important that will define the success of the organization over time. According to the Gartner Group, at least 40 percent of Fortune 1000 companies have implemented the balanced scorecard. The Harvard Business Review selected the balanced scorecard as one of the most influential business ideas of the past 75 years.

The same balanced scorecard that has been successfully used to measure progress in the business can be used to measure progress in Information Systems. In fact, a report by META predicting trends in the IT Performance Engineering and Measurement Strategies stated that during 1999 and 2000, an increasing awareness of the information systems link to business performance would encourage the use of information systems scorecards to monitor contributions to the business. By 2001 and 2002, they predicted that the dynamics of business would force more than half of the scorecards to evolve into dashboards that track information systems performance against investments and market share. They predicted that information systems dashboards would be used at all levels through 2003.

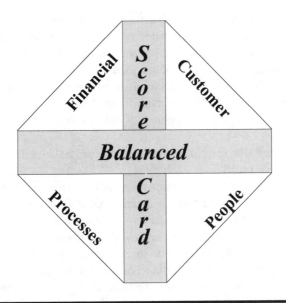

Figure 3.8 Balanced Scorecard Areas

Relative to an information systems scorecard, the four areas are shown in Figure 3.8 and described below.

- **Financial:** How much money is spent on Information Systems? Where is the money being spent? How much money is spent keeping the business functioning (e.g., legacy systems) versus moving the business forward (e.g., meeting the top business priorities)? How much revenue is generated from Information Systems initiatives (including e-commerce)? How does Information Systems look to senior management?

- **Customer:** How does Information Systems look to its customers (or users)? How satisfied are the customers? How well is Information Systems meeting service level agreements? With customers concerned about time, quality, performance, service, and cost, how much does Information Systems impact the end customer (including customer relationship management applications)?

- **Internal Process:** What are the internal process drivers of value? How well are the information systems processes formalized, documented, followed, and measured? How is time being spent within the Information Systems organization? How does Information Systems impact the business processes (including the entire supply chain management)? How does our execution compare to industry standards?

■ **Organizational Learning and Process Improvement (People):**
What is the ability of the Information Systems organization to learn
and improve? How well does the group keep pace with changing
technology? Are career plans formalized? What are the skills and
training that are required? What recruiting and retention programs
are implemented? How satisfied are the employees? Are we posi-
tioned to meet the challenges of the future?

Figure 3.9 shows the four information systems balanced scorecard areas
with examples of metrics in each area.

The information systems environment is constantly changing. At times,
it seems priorities can change on a daily basis and conflict among each
other. An information systems balanced scorecard can help focus on the
few things that really need to be achieved to produce the desired results.
The scorecard can help balance financial measures, such as information
systems expenditures as a percentage of sales, with operational measures,
such as customer satisfaction and system availability. It can expose the
whole picture among conflicting goals, such as achieving maximum customer satisfaction, implementing standard software packages, reducing
costs, improving quality, delivering projects on time, and retaining employees. The balanced scorecard can help set individual and team goals,
allocate resources, compensate employees, and plan budgets. It can provide feedback on an ongoing basis as to how individuals and departments
are performing in each area that has been identified as critical. A balanced
scorecard can help provide the focus necessary for an Information Systems
organization that is in a constant firefighting mode. It can also be a
powerful change management tool, because everyone in the organization
feels a sense of ownership and sees its value.

Implementing an information systems balanced scorecard is not an
event, but an entire process that could have implications in all the
processes within Information Systems. Figure 3.10 outlines the steps to
follow to implement an information systems balanced scorecard as
described below.

1. **Define Strategies:** Define and obtain agreement throughout the
   business and information systems on the short- and long-term strategies as part of the information systems strategic planning effort.
2. **Identify Critical Processes:** Identify which processes are critical
   to achieving the goals.
3. **Determine Metrics:** Determine the best ways to measure the effectiveness and efficiencies of those processes. These become the key
   performance indicators to track.

Financial	Customer	Internal	People
What:	***What:***	***What:***	***What:***
• Project and business area financial management • IS investment reporting • Financial management based on a business case	• Service level agreement (SLA) definition and reporting • Customer service satisfaction (CSS) survey • User certification	• Proactive management • Formal business process definitions • Project planning, management and reporting • Time tracking	• IS career plans • Employee continuous improvement • Recruiting and retention programs • Skills transitioning
Metrics:	***Metrics:***	***Metrics:***	***Metrics:***
• Percent of projects delivered within budget • Total (and by arcs) IS expense budget versus actual • Total IS capital budget versus actual • IS expense as a percent of sales • Percent of IS spending on legacy systems (keeping business functioning), including cost by system • Percent of spending on top business priorities (moving the business forward) • Sales revenue generated by IS initiatives • ROI by project	• Customer satisfaction survey results • Percent of projects delivered that achieve business benefits which were identified • Percent of applications under SLA's • Percent of SLA compliance • Call volume by application and root cause • Percent of calls resolved by time slice • Percent of calls generated by user group • Percent of user participation by project • Percent of requests serviced by users	• Percent of projects delivered on time • Median time to market for change or system • Average length of time problem report is open • Number of projects budgeted versus actually delivered • Percent of areas using formal methods and processes • Percent of applications that are custom compared to package software • Number of modifications to package software • Number of defects after production • Backlog of change requests • Percent of software on current release	• Employee satisfaction survey results • Annual IS turnover (total and by cause) • Average tenure • Overtime per month by skill level • Percent of employees in support, management, maintenance, and development roles • Span of control • Percent of contractors to employees • Average training hours by skill level • Average time positions are open • Number of open positions • Number of off-hours support calls • Number of telecommuters • Number of internal promotions

Figure 3.9 Closed Loop Measurement

4. **Track Metrics:** Identify and implement changes necessary to track the identified metrics. This may require technology, reports, or other changes.

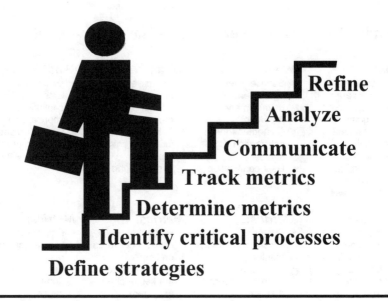

Figure 3.10 Steps to Implement an IS Balanced Scorecard

5. **Communicate:** Communicate the scorecard and metrics throughout the organization.
6. **Analyze:** Analyze and communicate the results on a regular basis. Celebrate success and identify areas to improve as needed.
7. **Refine:** Refine or revisit the metrics on a regular basis to ensure they continue to reflect the information systems strategic direction, as this will change over time.

Following are factors to consider in developing a balanced scorecard:

■ Is there a strategic vision? If the strategic vision is not clear, it is difficult to find the correct measurements.
■ Do we have management buy-in and support? The CIO and business executives must understand and believe in (and want) the measurements.
■ Do measurements and initiatives tie to our strategy? If they do not tie, too many resources are expended on activities that will not contribute to success. Ensure the scorecard is strategic in nature, not just operational or tactical.
■ Does the compensation program tie to the strategy? Reward individuals for obtaining strategic initiatives and for improving the metrics. If there is no reward, motivation to change will be reduced.
■ Does a purpose exist for implementing the scorecard? Does the proper environment exist? For example, the middle of downsizing

Figure 3.11 Balanced Scorecard Example

and stretching the organization may not be a good time to implement a new scorecard. Although it can provide much needed focus for the organization, the change may be too much to absorb.

- Are the scorecard, its importance, and the measures communicated to every level of the organization, including within and outside of Information Systems?
- Are measurements revisited to confirm their relevance to the updated information systems strategic direction? This is an ongoing learning and changing process.

Figure 3.11 shows an example of a balanced scorecard used by one company.

Figure 3.12 shows another example of an information systems balanced scorecard. The company using this one tied its specific initiatives to the target, measure, and objective within the four perspectives of the balanced scorecard. This company also analyzed the cause-and-effect linkages

Perspective	Objective	Measure	Target	Initiative	
Financial	Sales Growth - 10% Net Operating Profit After Tax (NOPAT) - 12-15% NOPAT/ NetAssets - TBD	Rapid response time Highly available systems Easily available sales info Reduce cost of maint - Simplify environment - Insturment applications - Solve root causes Optimize use of Systems - Simplify environment - Gather usage metrics	Response time < n secs Systems available — 99% Reduce the number of platforms to n1	Simplify Standardize Integrate Automate	
Customer	Deliver new, flexible systems Easy access to actionable information Systems available when needed Deliver business productivity tools	Customer satisfaction Service Level Agreements Hits on web site Number of problems w/ automated response	90% 7 × 24 Increasing Increasing	e-business Global Data Warehouse Batch to BMP Database Upgrade Notes Implementation PDM Implementation	SDLC ISSC Reeng Consol/scrub data MRP Configurator Kanban
Internal Processes	Simplify/Standardize Computing Environment Provide browser access to data Formalize processes Capture knowledge Keep systems current Maintain business systems	Number of PC Software Packages Percent of systems accessible via browser Percent of processes reengineered/formalized Number of knowledge bases Percent of PCs replaced Maintenance levels of sfw System utilization Size of the problem log	Decreasing Increasing Increasing Increasing 25% <1 year and >6 months of current <70% Decreasing	Service desk (Case-Based Reasoning, CBT) Disributed monitoring (Servers, S/390, Apps) Tivoli reporting (Service Desk, Inventory) Process identification, Documentation, Reengineering Network maintenance/Upgrade (FrameRelay, ATM, 100M Hubs) Software Maintenance/Upgrade (PC, AIX, OS/390) Hardware maintenance/Upgrade (PC Servers, S/390)	
Learning & Growth	Skilled employees Employee satisfaction	Hours training Employee turnover	80 hours/ employee <5%	Training program (Java, . . .) Competitive salaries/benefits	

Figure 3.12 Information Systems Balanced Scorecard Example

between the objectives by drawing them across the four balanced scorecard areas. This analysis is shown in Figure 3.13. This diagram outlines the relationships among the objectives, which can be helpful in determining the impact of various changes.

Metrics Evolution

The metrics might grow and need to be modified as progression is made through the process evolution stages that were presented in Chapter 1. Figure 3.14 shows how the focus of the metrics may change as a company

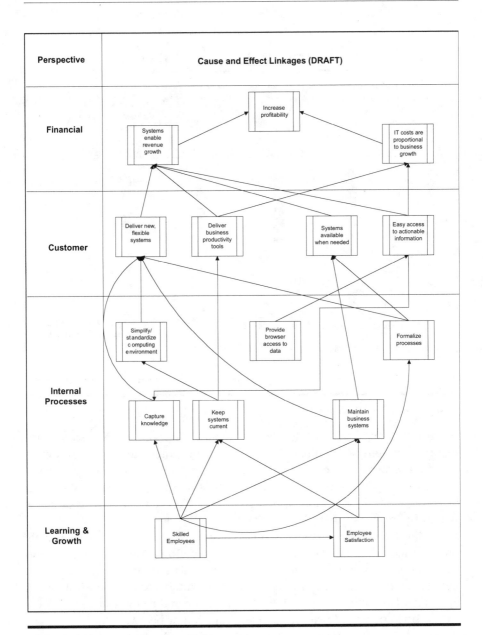

Figure 3.13 Cause and Effect Linkages

moves through the stages of process evolution. A company in the firefighting stage would have few, if any, metrics.

A company in the second stage, Desire, might focus on the operational efficiencies of Information Systems, providing the services faster and cheaper. They would focus on reducing expenses. The Information Systems

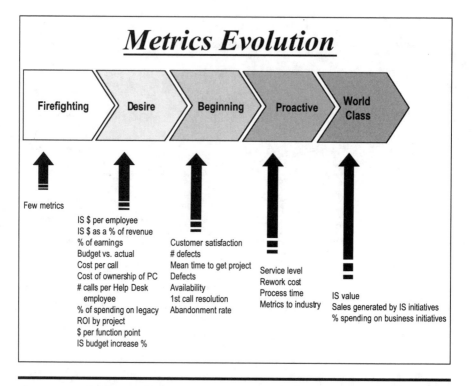

Figure 3.14 Metrics Evolution

budget and expenses would receive much attention. Extra systems and expenses would be eliminated. Ongoing management discipline and measurement processes are instituted in this stage. The power is in the process and the discipline. Tools to analyze and report the operational data might be implemented. Communication to staff and management on the progress would be important based on the goals and metrics.

In the third stage, Beginning, Information Systems would focus heavily on a service orientation. In addition to the operational metrics in the second stage, a company in this stage would be particularly interested in improved delivery and execution. Customer satisfaction would become a critical metric and focus. Communication and dialog both from and to Information Systems would be important. Customer focus groups might be formed.

In the Proactive stage, Information Systems would become a key component to the business. There would be additional metrics important to those presented in the previous stages. A balanced scorecard might be implemented. Benchmarking would become a regular practice. Trend analysis of data would be critical to proactively identify issues. Service level agreements would be in place. Rewards would be tied to the measures. Relationship management and proactive communication with the business units would be critical.

In the World Class stage, Information Systems would be integrated with the business and with the business results. The business measures would become the Information Systems measures. Information Systems would be involved in defining the business strategy. There would be a focus on measuring the value of Information Systems. Information Systems would be run like a business and mirror the way the business operates. The business leaders would present and be responsible for the success of the Information Systems projects and status. The business would project the use of Information Systems as part of the business planning cycle. An Information Systems account manager might be assigned to each business unit in a large company.

Process Improvement Goals

With an understanding that the metrics may change as the company proceeds through the evolution stages, we need to think about where the organization is on the evolution scale and the specific process improvement goals. Process improvement goals are determined by the proper metrics for the organization, which reflect the organization's priorities and direction. The targets and metrics are determined by simply selecting the metrics that will assist in meeting the objectives, through a balanced scorecard approach or through benchmarking. We now know what is important and the precise target we are striving for as processes are improved within Information Systems. We must keep in mind that, according to The Standish Group International in 1998, 6 percent of projects fail due to unrealistic expectations, and 5 percent of all projects fail due to unclear objectives. If the process improvement goals are not clear, we must go back through the strategic plan and metrics — it is critical. Whatever the goal is in initiating process improvement, we need to make sure that the metrics measured are reflective of that goal.

UNDERSTAND THE IS ENVIRONMENT

It is important to understand the environment and culture in the company and within the Information Systems organization, as it can significantly impact the ability to implement a process improvement methodology. The culture will also impact the speed at which the organization can evolve through the various stages of process evolution described earlier. Environmental factors are important to understand, as they may impact time and many other items, such as:

- The level of effort and size of project that will be required to implement a process culture
- The cost to implement a process culture
- The level of success

- The level of opportunities for improvement which will be realized in a new environment
- The amount of encouragement and management support that may be necessary
- The amount of training that will be required
- The way to organize the project and the steps to take to implement a process improvement culture
- The level of acceptance the culture will have for the changes
- The amount of turnover that may be experienced as a result of the changes
- The communication plan that may be necessary during the change process
- The size and composition of the process control team
- Organizational changes which may be necessary
- The degree of change which may be necessary

The readiness assessment tool outlined in Appendix C may be used to help evaluate the culture in the Information Systems organization.

ESTABLISH THE STEERING TEAM

Now that the high-level vision of where we want to be with improved processes has been established, we must establish the process improvement steering team that will guide the effort and be responsible for guiding the overall process improvement. Although other individuals in the organization will be involved as we focus on each particular process, it is this core steering team that will ensure consistency across processes and coordinate processes across organizational boundaries. The team will think about, understand, and question everything. Following are suggested requirements when forming the steering team:

- It is best to have individuals who have open minds, can think outside of the box, and are not resistant to change.
- It is good to have a mix of individuals: some that know (or work in) the processes that will have the major emphasis; some who are currently not close to the process so they can provide a fresh perspective; some who are customers of, or provide input into, the processes that will be the main focus; and some who have been with the organization a long time as well as those fairly new to the organization.
- Having some external consultants should be considered. Consultants can be useful to provide best-in-class examples, provide a fresh perspective, and provide process knowledge, particularly if this is a new concept to the organization.

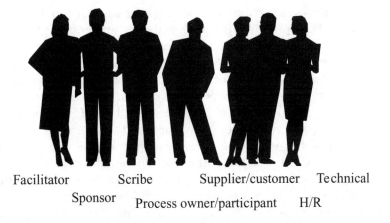

Facilitator   Scribe   Supplier/customer   Technical
        Sponsor   Process owner/participant   H/R

Figure 3.15 Process Steering Team

- Individuals from the various functional areas of the organization need to be involved.
- During the implementation, it is helpful if the individuals are influential within the organization.
- Individuals who support process methodology and process concepts should be on the team.

The steering team may be a diverse group of individuals, but they are brought together with a common goal and vision of the future. After identifying the participants, the team members, as well as the particular roles and responsibilities for each member, are documented. Some things to consider when thinking about the roles and responsibilities:

- Will the steering team members facilitate the process improvement efforts throughout the Information Systems organization as well as be responsible for designing and implementing the new processes?
- Will they be responsible for leading simultaneous process improvement efforts?
- What is their role in implementation?
- What is their role after implementation?

Following are roles and responsibilities to consider when forming the steering team, as shown in Figure 3.15:

- **Sponsor:** The sponsor establishes the vision for the future. The sponsor communicates the purpose of the reengineering effort as a whole and what benefits are hoped to be achieved. He or she has the passion and motivation to make the reengineering efforts survive through the tough times. The sponsor must have authority and responsibility to get resources, involvement, decisions made, and commitment.

■ **Facilitator:** The facilitator ensures a productive environment for the process steering team. The facilitator is the catalyst who helps the team members think outside of the box while also keeping the discussion on task. It is best if this person is a neutral party not directly impacted by the processes.

■ **Process Owners:** One or two of the process owners of some of the critical processes should be included on the team.

■ **Suppliers:** Individuals who provide input into some of the key information systems processes should be included on the team.

■ **Customers:** Individuals who use the output from some of the key information systems processes, should be represented on the team.

■ **Process Participants:** A few of the knowledgeable, supportive participants in the key processes should be members of the team.

■ **Technical Participants:** Some of the key technical resource personnel who will be involved in implementing key pieces of technology that may be necessary should be included on the team. They would have a high level of understanding of the technology that is available, the impact of various emerging technologies, and the effort involved in implementing certain technologies.

■ **Human Resources:** Someone to represent the human and cultural aspects of the process improvement effort should be considered for the team.

■ **Scribe:** The scribe is responsible for taking and distributing notes from all the meetings and discussions. This includes following up on action items to ensure closure.

The time commitment expected from the team members should be documented, making sure to adjust priorities so that they can dedicate the time necessary to complete the project successfully. According to the Standish Group International, Inc., study in 1998, six percent of all projects failed due to a lack of resources and eight percent due to a lack of executive support. The team must have enough of the right resources to be successful.

DEVELOP THE PROJECT PLAN

We are now ready to document the plans and intentions for the overall process improvement project in a formal project plan document. This will ensure that everyone understands the game plan, including the goals, objectives, schedule, roles, and responsibilities. The project should be planned in whole and executed in parts.

Case for Action

A key component of the project plan is building the Case for Action for process improvement. Guidelines follow for developing a Case for Action.

- It is a compelling, clear, believable, and concise argument for why the organization would invest the resources to improve processes.
- It is not lengthy (approximately one page). It does not require intensive communication to understand the information.
- It states the need for dramatic improvements. It does not scold or assign blame, but rather frames the need for improvements.
- It identifies how the organization currently looks in the eyes of your customers.
- It identifies what the organization must become, the vision of how things ought to be.
- It identifies why the processes must be restructured and supports the argument with facts and data, if possible. For example, the need may be due to survival, growth, or security reasons.
- The statements should generate passion and persuade people that there is no other alternative. It is personalized so every individual feels responsibility for changing. The fear of not changing must be greater than the fear of changing.
- It may identify satisfying the customer as the driving force in the Case for Action.

The components to include in the Case for Action are:

- **Environment:** What is happening in the Information Systems environment or what has changed to cause concern
- **Problem:** The source of the concerns
- **Demands:** Customer expectations, described in detail
- **Diagnosis:** Why the current methods are unable to meet the demands
- **Cost of Inaction:** What the consequence of staying status quo are
- **Objective:** What the guiding goals that will indicate success are

An example of a Case for Action is shown in Figure 3.16.

Contents of Plan

The process improvement project is just like any other information systems project and needs the following items to be successful:

**Overall Information Systems Process Improvement
Case for Action**

Business Environment:
Competitive pressures, growth objectives, and customer demands made it necessary for our company to enter into e-business.

Business Problem:
The problem is that our information systems support processes are not designed to support the new e-business strategy.

Demands of the Marketplace:
To be effective and meet the customer demands in the e-business environment, our systems must be reliable, stable, accurate, quick to change, and integrated.

Diagnosis:
Our current information systems methods are unable to meet the new expectations because our processes are not consistent, not documented, not efficient, not streamlined, and not integrated. In fact, we don't have processes at all, as each issue is handled and solved individually in a fire-fighting, reactive mode. Specific inefficient and ineffective processes which directly impact the delivery of information systems in support of the e-business environment include: Change Management, Performance and Availability Management, Backup and Disaster Recovery Management, Service Level Management, and Systems Development Processes.

Cost of Inaction:
The only thing worse than no e-business presence is a bad e-business presence. Our systems now directly impact the end customer. Due to issues with our cumbersome processes, our systems are experiencing unnecessary down time and not meeting the changing needs of the business. This down time can result in lost customers, lost revenue, and bad publicity in the market. Systems that are slow to change could impact our ability to remain competitive and impact our market share. Inability to improve information systems processes could jeopardize our very survival as a company.

Objective:
Our objectives of the information systems process improvement effort is to improve system availability by 25 percent, and decrease the mean time to complete systems enhancements by 25 percent.

Figure 3.16 Case for Action Example

- A well-defined focus
- Clear, obtainable vision and objectives
- Sense of urgency, a specific due date with realistic time frames
- Involvement from the organization
- Executive management support
- Training to support the new methods and technology
- Proper planning
- Small project milestones
- Clearly defined requirements
- A competent team that owns the project
- Sufficient resources

A checklist to ensure that the process improvement project (or any other project) has the right components for success is included in Appendix D.

Now that the Case for Action has been developed, people are inspired to act. We must now outline the action, including the following items in the project plan document:

- **Project Mission:** What the effort is trying to accomplish
- **Project Scope:** What areas of information systems processes will be included and what will be excluded
- **Project Goals:** What the specific metrics that will be utilized to measure progress in the Information Systems organization are and how success will be defined
- **Case for Action:** Why improvement is necessary
- **Project Team Organization:** Who will be involved and how much time will be necessary for the project
- **Roles and Responsibilities:** The specific responsibilities for each member on the team
- **Methodology:** Any particular methodology that will be followed, including what automated tools (such as charting software) that the team will use
- **Tasks and Deliverables:** The tasks necessary to complete the improvement project and who will be responsible for completion of the tasks
- **Schedule:** The schedule and time frame for completion of tasks

Managing the Information Systems process improvement effort as a project will improve the odds of success. It will ensure that resources dedicate the proper amount of time and that tasks stay on track. The project plan will move the organization to action.

PROCESS TRAINING

Process improvement is a new concept to many Information Systems organizations. We may get blank stares when even talking about processes to Information Systems individuals, due to the unique and firefighting nature of the business. Before beginning the project, it is critical that everyone is grounded in process methodology with a common understanding and vocabulary. Whatever methodology is chosen for the improvement effort, the team must be educated in the methodology, tools, and process fundamentals.

PITFALLS TO AVOID

In the Getting Started step, there are a few pitfalls to avoid:

- **Inability to get started:** It is always easiest to delay process improvement. "We have too much on our plate at this time. We'll get started in three months." How often have we heard that? Three months goes by, and there are more initiatives and projects to distract our attention. When companies are in the firefighting mode, it can be very difficult to carve out time to improve how work is being done. Avoiding this pitfall takes a strong management commitment. Process improvement must consistently be identified as a priority. Even if as many resources as desired cannot be dedicated, some progress is better than no progress. The organization must be trained in process improvement methods and the value in improving processes. We must build a Case for Action to convince the organization why it is important.

- **Not obtaining proper management support and commitment:** At times it may be only individuals within the organization who recognize the need for process improvement. Management may not be aware, understand the need, or see the problems as process problems. Although the processes may be able to be improved within one area, management support is necessary because processes need resources and they typically cross organizational boundaries. We must educate management in the value of process improvement, write a business Case for Action on why it is important, and present a proposal to management. Without management support, it is difficult to make the culture changes that need to occur and have a sustaining effort with resources committed to the effort.

- **Not obtaining proper resources and not adjusting priorities:** Particularly in a firefighting mode, it is easy to throw the process improvement expectations on top of the organization with all the other priorities and requirements. Oftentimes, this leads to no progress and a frustrated organization. Process improvement needs to be an identified project with hours and resources committed to it. Other priorities must be adjusted to accommodate the expectations. As new priorities are highlighted each day, the prioritization process must take into account the resources allocated to process improvement. Scheduling standing process improvement meetings with assignments is one way to keep the focus.

- **Lack of vision of where the effort is leading:** Many times when we start talking about process improvement to the organization, many individuals may not understand the concepts or the vision where we want them to be. Communication and training are critical. We must continually communicate the vision of how the department should function. Having specific metrics or a balanced scorecard is a good way for individuals to know the vision and exactly where they are in the journey. A final destination must be clearly defined and communicated so the entire organization can work toward the objective and direction.

- **Ambiguous action plans:** Once training is completed and the vision is clear, then steps or action plans with responsibilities need to be identified. Each process is assigned to a particular individual and/or team of individuals to improve. They should have guidance through the process if they are new to process improvement. Consulting and external assistance can be very helpful.

- **Lack of training:** The group must have sufficient training on process improvement methodologies. There is nothing more frustrating for some individuals than to know where they need to be, but not know how to get there. Some individuals may require more training than others. We must frequently support the journey; obtain books, training courses, and articles; and continually look for new training and ideas.

KEY POINTS TO REMEMBER

- Process objectives should be derived from the information systems strategic plan and the business plan.
- An information systems balanced scorecard can be an effective way to measure progress.
- The process improvement effort should be treated like any other project. Establish a process steering committee, understand the environment, develop a project plan, determine objectives, and obtain training.
- A Case for Action must be developed to inspire the organization to improve the processes.
- Deliverables from the first step, Getting Started, include:
  - Interview notes
  - Observation summary
  - Project plan with Case for Action, team, roles, responsibilities, methodology, tasks, and schedule
  - Process workshop training

NOTES AND IDEAS FOR MY PROCESS IMPROVEMENT EFFORT

4

PROCESS IDENTIFICATION

"The most effective way to cope with change is to help create it."

L.W. Lynett

Now that we have started and organized the project, the second step in the process improvement effort is Process Identification. In this step, all the processes that are performed within the Information Systems organization will be identified. The following tasks will be completed:

- **Understand Area:** Gaining a good understanding of the entire Information Systems area, interviewing individuals and understanding current activities, tasks, inputs, and outputs
- **Identify Processes:** Identifying current processes that are utilized in the Information Systems organization, understanding the interfaces among the various processes
- **Document Description:** Describing each process to document the purpose, or why the process exists
- **Identify Benefits:** Identifying the benefits of having the process, determining if the process is necessary to have
- **Identify Issues:** Identifying high-level issues that currently exist with the process

These steps are shown in Figure 4.1. Each of these tasks will be discussed in more detail.

UNDERSTAND INFORMATION SYSTEMS AREA

Before trying to identify specific processes, we need to have a good idea of what goes on in the Information Systems environment. We can't improve

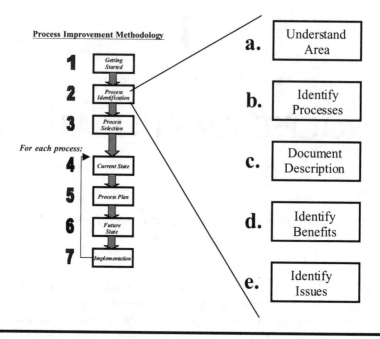

Figure 4.1 Process Identification

what we don't know. It can be very helpful to interview individuals within Information Systems to gain a better understanding of what they do. The following are questions to ask:

- What are your specific roles and responsibilities?
- What do you spend your time on during a typical day? What activities do you do?
- How do you do them?
- Why do you do them?
- What input do you receive from other areas?
- What output do you provide other areas?
- Do you use any particular technology?
- How is the work directed, scheduled, performed, and controlled?
- How does the activity interact with others?
- Do you have any special activities to do on a weekly basis? Monthly? Yearly?
- How do the activities support achieving objectives?
- How do you measure your effectiveness and efficiency?
- What issues do you have with what you do?
- How could you be more effective and efficient?

Since processes typically evolve around things or information that moves, we are trying to find out what moves through or within the department, asking good probing questions and following up on the responses to understand why things are done a certain way.

IDENTIFY INFORMATION SYSTEMS PROCESSES

Now that we have a good general understanding of the work performed in the department, we are ready to identify the specific processes. We need to get a group of key individuals together to identify the processes, begining with listing the activities that were identified as being performed within the Information Systems organization, then grouping the activities into processes, and finally grouping the processes into major areas. Processes will cross organizational boundaries, so we must not be limited in thinking by organizational silos. It is very helpful to document the processes in a diagram known as a high-level process map or model.

Figure 4.2 is an important figure that can be used as a starting point in process identification. The figure identifies the common processes found in a typical Information Systems organization and displays them in a high-level process map or model. This process model will be used throughout the remainder of this book to refer to the information systems processes. For each process listed, the book will provide:

- Process descriptions
- Process benefits
- Process issues
- Process design components

Keep in mind that the processes identified for a particular organization may be slightly different from those identified in the process model shown in Figure 4.2. It is important to get individuals together who know the organization to identify the specific processes rather than to adopt a generic model. The processes have been grouped into the following areas:

- **Manage Systems:** The processes necessary to develop, maintain, and manage the systems, including the hardware, software, and network environments
- **Manage Business Applications:** The processes required to develop and maintain the business application environment
- **Manage Business Relationships:** Processes that interface Information Systems with the business customers and create a positive collaborative relationship

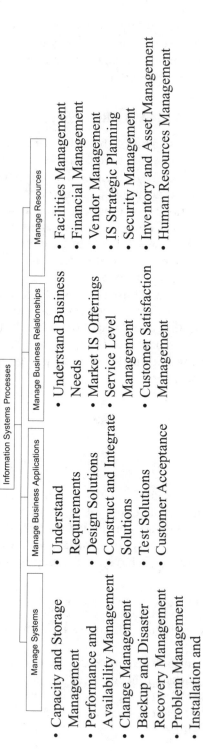

Figure 4.2 Typical Information Systems Processes

■ **Manage Resources:** Processes required to manage all Information Systems resources, including people, facilities, finances, equipment, and software

After identifying the processes within the organization, there are typically many relationships and interfaces to be found among these processes. Drawing a diagram will help to identify the interfaces among the various processes to see their interrelationships and dependencies. The following processes interface information with just about every other process and are, therefore, key processes that are in the core of Information Systems:

■ IS Strategic Planning Process
■ Service Level Management Process
■ Inventory and Asset Management Process
■ Installation and Configuration Management Process
■ Capacity and Storage Management Process
■ Change Management Process
■ Problem Management Process
■ Performance and Availability Management Process

In fact, research done by The Meta Group (7/30/98 identifying trends for 2000) identified processes such as Problem Management, Change Management, Inventory and Asset Management, and Service Level Management to be crucial processes in how users perceive the Information Systems organization. Meta said that these critical processes should be designed as part of the information systems architecture as they are so integrated and integral to how Information Systems delivers service to its customers.

The interrelationships among the processes must be carefully managed. There must be crossfunctional process integration, so there are single stores of information and the group is solution-oriented. For example, the Inventory and Asset Management Process and the Software Distribution Management Process both have the same number of PCs accounted for in a company. Another example is that both the Capacity and Storage Management Process and the Performance and Availability Management Process strive for the same service levels which are agreed to in the service level management process. An example of a process interface map is shown in Figure 4.3.

DOCUMENT DESCRIPTION

Next, the description of each of the processes needs to be documented. What activities or functions individuals perform often translate to the

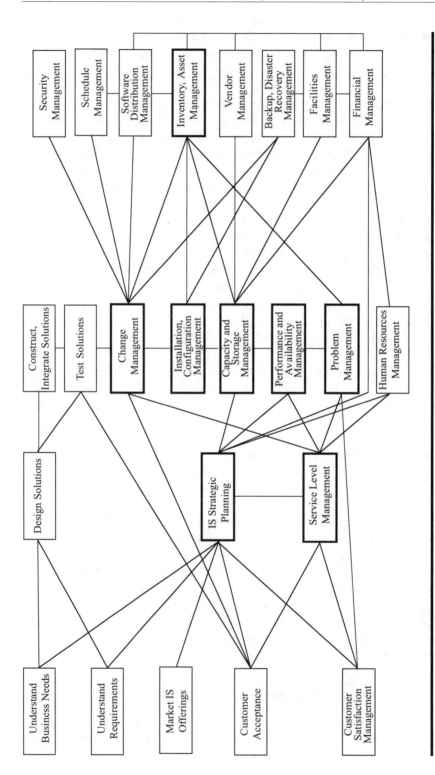

Figure 4.3 Process Interface Map

description of the process. Appendix E shows each of the processes that have been identified in the process model and their descriptions. The process descriptions, process names, and process areas in each environment may be slightly different.

IDENTIFY BENEFITS

Next, the benefits of having the process must be identified. Through this effort, we need to discuss or determine whether the process is necessary at all, remembering that one way to improve a process is to eliminate it. Processes may be developed to fill a particular need, which may become obsolete over time, but the process remains because that is the way things have always been done. An example of benefits for the Information Systems processes that were identified is shown in Appendix F.

IDENTIFY ISSUES

Next, we must identify at a high level some of the issues that may be occurring within the processes. It is important to identify the high-level issues rather than the details of the process. For example, having information on-line rather than on a report refers to details within the process, whereas a high-level process issue may be that a process is not always used consistently. An example of possible issues that may occur within the processes that were identified earlier is included in Appendix G.

PITFALLS TO AVOID

In this second step, process identification, there are several pitfalls to avoid:

- **Lack of involvement:** Especially during the first three steps of the process, we need to involve as many people from the organization as possible and not try to do this step alone. No matter how well we know the organization, we can obtain tremendous value by involving others and adding other perspectives. Other priorities must be structured so key individuals can participate.
- **Requiring total consensus:** When working with a team, some people feel a need to obtain total consensus before proceeding. This may not always be possible. For example, when identifying issues within a process, one individual may insist that something is an issue, while another person (perhaps someone involved in the process) may believe it is not an issue. It is important to remember that perception is reality. Consensus is not necessary.

If something is an issue for one person, it is probably an issue. We must establish ground rules up-front on how the team will function, encourage input and involvement, and not stifle creativity and thinking outside the box.

■ **Requiring perfection:** It is very easy to get stuck in analysis paralysis and strive for 100 percent perfection. Typically the last 5 percent of perfection is not worth the time and effort required to obtain it. Instead, we need to utilize an iterative approach where the processes are implemented and refined based on feedback. Nothing has to be final; we can continually go back and add or change. With an iterative approach, the need for perfection is reduced before moving on.

■ **Thinking of processes within an organizational silo:** To look at a complete process, we must cross organizational boundaries if needed. Otherwise some of the major opportunities for improvement may be missed. Usually it is at the points where the process crosses organizations where there is a tremendous amount of waste and the ball can get dropped. The process improvement team must consist of individuals involved in the process from beginning to end, not just from one department.

■ **Turf issues:** A tricky part of process improvement is to throw politics and turf issues out the window. Improvement can be severely hampered by individuals scared to change, scared to give up responsibility or personnel, or looking to further their own advancement. Communication is critical so that all participants feel valued and not threatened. We must convey to participants that process improvement will make them more effective and allow them to have more challenging responsibilities. If individuals feel that their jobs will be threatened by improving the process, we can expect nothing but resistance.

KEY POINTS TO REMEMBER

■ To identify processes, we must understand the environment first, looking for physical and information movement within the department, asking *why* five times to get down to the true meaning.

■ Processes will cross organizational boundaries, don't think in organizational silos when identifying processes.

■ We must be aware of and carefully manage the relationships among the processes.

■ A process description answers *what*, while process benefits answer *why*. Issues identify what is wrong.

- ■ Deliverables from the second step, Process Identification, include:
  - ■ Process overview map containing all the processes
  - ■ Process documentation
  - ■ Purpose
  - ■ Benefits
  - ■ Issues

NOTES AND IDEAS FOR MY PROCESS IMPROVEMENT EFFORT

5

PROCESS SELECTION

"The difficulty in life is choice."

George Moore

With an understanding of how to identify processes, we now proceed to the next step which is to select the best process to work on. Is it better to work on the Problem Management Process or the Performance and Availability Process? Or, perhaps it is best to work on the Understand Requirements Process or the Inventory and Asset Management Process. Determining the best process to work on can be difficult, especially when the selection needs to be justified. Therefore, we need to use a defined methodology to select, prioritize, and support the process decision. The methodology used to select processes is shown in Figure 5.1 and is described as follows:

- **Analyze Value:** Processes need to be analyzed for value before being prioritized and selected.
- **Prioritize Processes:** Once the value is established, each process can be prioritized based on set criteria.
- **Select Processes:** Using one of several techniques, the prioritized processes can be selected for change.

ANALYZE VALUE

Each process in the Information Systems organization supports an area of the business, the information system itself, or the enterprise applications. The extent to which the process supports these business areas is important to understand. As shown in Figure 5.2 and described below, there are seven key process values in the Information Systems organization.

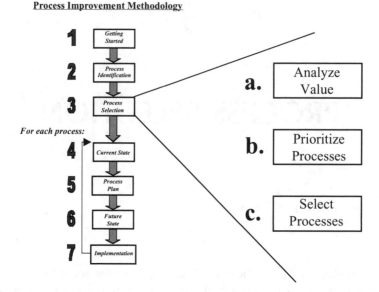

Figure 5.1 Process Selection

- **Generates revenue:** The degree to which the process generates revenue for the organization
- **Contains costs:** The degree to which the process contributes to cost containment
- **Improves productivity:** The degree to which the process improves the productivity of people throughout the organization
- **Supports strategy:** The degree to which the process supports the company's information systems plan, business plan, or departmental plan
- **Ensures operations:** The degree to which the process supports the recovery of information services supporting critical applications
- **Improves flexibility:** The degree to which the process enables the organization to be responsive to changing business conditions
- **Integrates technology:** The degree to which the process supports other information systems processes and applications critical to the functions of the business

Although these values provide a foundation for selecting processes, not all processes provide the same kind of value for all companies. For example, the Backup and Disaster Recovery Management Process does not support the ability to generate revenue in a traditional manufacturing company. But to a dot-com online shopping company this process is

Generates revenue

Integrates technology

Contains costs

Improves flexibility

Improves productivity

Ensures operations

Supports strategy

Figure 5.2 Process Values

critical in supporting the ability to generate revenue. The degree by which a process supports a specific business value can vary. It can significantly support, somewhat support, or not support a value. These three levels are defined as follows.

- **Significantly supports:** The main intent and purpose of the process is to support a given business value; for example, the Backup and Disaster Recovery process significantly supports the value of continued operations.
- **Somewhat supports:** The process is designed to provide ok results; for example, Backup and Disaster Recovery somewhat supports the value of improved productivity.
- **Does not support:** The process does not support in any manner a particular business value; for example, Backup and Disaster Recovery does not directly support the strategic direction.

Figure 5.3 shows a value analysis for the Inventory and Asset Management Process. Besides determining a level of value for the process, the figure also demonstrates how one can attach simple numeric weights (such as *0* for none, *5* for somewhat, and *10* for significant) to each level and objectively determine the value of that specific process to the business. In our example, the Inventory and Asset Management Process has a value rating of 20. Repeating this weighting for each of the information system processes creates a value matrix to guide the process efforts.

Value analysis helps prioritize processes. It focuses attention on processes most important to the organization. The values listed in this example may need to change depending on the company and environment. Whatever the final list, value analysis should be performed on each process before any selection occurs.

Inventory and Asset Management Process			
Business Value	*Support Level*		
	0 pts None	5 pts Somewhat	10 pts Significant
Generates Revenue	X		
Contains Costs			X
Improves Productivity		X	
Supports Strategy	X		
Ensures Operations	X		
Improves Flexibility		X	
Integrates Technology	X		
	Rating = 20 points		

Figure 5.3 Value Analysis Example

PRIORITIZE PROCESSES

There are many different techniques to prioritize processes. It is important to select a prioritization technique that fits the particular environment. Some environments are very formal and structured. The prioritization process should therefore be driven by data and analytically sound. Other environments are very open and fluid. The prioritization process in this environment needs to engage people in discussion and consensus. Some environments are in between these two examples. As shown in Figure 5.4 and discussed below, there are five approaches to prioritizing processes, and each of these is outlined in detail.

Criteria-Based Approach

The criteria-based approach of prioritizing processes is data driven and most useful to minimize the impact of people and personalities influencing the priorities. Initially, the criteria-based approach may be difficult to establish due to its numerical rating base. However, once established, this approach clearly identifies where process attention should be placed.

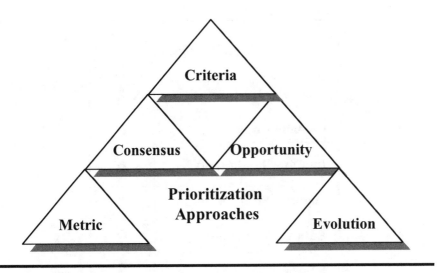

Figure 5.4 Prioritization Approaches

To establish a criteria-based approach, we need to discuss with various business leaders what impact and value information systems have on the business and use this input to create a listing of criteria by which to score each process. For example, to establish selection criteria, one company used the values discussed in the previous section. They listed these criteria across the top of the selection grid and used them to select processes to improve. Different companies may have slightly different criteria. Criteria should be selected to fit the particular management style and company culture.

Once determined, the criteria are prioritized by identifying a weight for the importance of each. Which is more important: to improve productivity or to contain costs? Or, is ensuring operations more important? The answer is not always straightforward. Depending on the business climate and the specific area being considered, the criteria may be weighted differently. Figure 5.5 shows an example of how the criteria were weighted for one company. A high number indicates that the criteria significantly impact the organization.

Next, each of the information systems processes that were previously identified (e.g., Problem Management, Asset and Inventory Management) is listed on the selection worksheet. Figure 5.6 shows an example of a process selection worksheet for several processes supporting the information systems function. With the processes listed, the impact each process can have on the criteria is rated. For example, if a change is made to the Inventory and Asset Management Process, what will the impact be on improving productivity? If it is a significant impact, score this process with a 10. If it will have no impact, it is scored with a 0. If it will have somewhat

Criteria Weighting	
Generates Revenue	**4**
Contains Costs	**10**
Improves Productivity	**6**
Supports Strategy	**7**
Ensures Operations	**9**
Improves Flexibility	**5**
Integrates Technology	**8**

Figure 5.5 Examples of Weighted Criteria

of an impact, it is scored in the middle. In this example, let us use the logic that an effective process will rotate assets and, therefore, keep the productivity levels somewhat current with technology. We score it a 5. Now for the same process, we proceed to ask the question with another criterion. For example, if a change is made to the Inventory and Asset Management Process, what will the impact be on containing costs? If our logic relates to better assignment and technology, the score will tend to be significant, perhaps an 8. We will continue to go through each process and score the process against each criterion and fill in the supporting data on the worksheet.

Next, we multiply the process impact times the criteria importance weighting. A 5 impact rating on a weighted criteria of 5 is a score of 25 (5×5). An 8 rating on a high weighted business cost impact of 10 yields a score of 80 (8×10). We continue this process until each process is compared and scored against the criteria. By considering the total ratings for each process, we can determine which processes are in need of changes.

The criteria approach is an effective analytical method to prioritizing and selecting processes. This numerically based model is used only as a guideline and needs to be adapted to fit a particular environment.

Process Area: Manage Systems Owner: *Mike H.* Date: **14th**

Criteria (weights shown in parentheses):

Processes	Generates Revenue	Contains Costs (4)	Improves Productivity (10)	Supports Strategy (6)	Ensures Operations (7)	Improves Flexibility (9)	(5)	Integrates Technology (8)	Total
Capacity and Storage Management	Transparent	Need to capture falling disk costs — 2 / 8	Currently Available — 9 / 90	Need more Real Time Access — 0 / 0	OK Provides Redundancy — 7 / 49	Transparent — 3 / 27	2 / 10	Need Enterprise Solution — 8 / 64	248
Performance and Availability Management	No need	Predictable now. OK — 1 / 4	Speed & Uptime OK — 2 / 20	OK Proactive — 2 / 12	Manages System OK Today — 2 / 14	Adequate — 0 / 0	0 / 0	Better if under one system — 8 / 64	114
Change Management	Need to improve Timeliness	Integrate better other changes — 6 / 24	Need to reduce transition time and impact — 7 / 70	To become more responsive, Dynamic — 6 / 36	Transparent impact — 8 / 56	For users, yes. More needed — 2 / 18	5 / 25	No opportunities — 0 / 0	229
Backup and Disaster Recovery Management	<4 hours no impact	Down currently costs $49K/Hr — 5 / 20	Need to ID and protect key loc. — 10 / 100	No unique support — 4 / 24	Need to shore up. Exposed. — 2 / 14	Allows interrupt functioning — 10 / 90	7 / 35	Not significant. Synchronizations — 3 / 24	307
Problem Management	No impact or need	Minimal — 0 / 0	User impact some — 1 / 10	Little impact on strategy — 3 / 18	From a user perspective OK — 0 / 0	Transparent — 1 / 9	0 / 0	Not applicable — 0 / 0	37
Installation and Configuration Mgt	No impact or need	Minimal — 0 / 0	Current — 1 / 10	No direct link — 2 / 12	Need to control Rev releases — 0 / 0	Transparent — 7 / 63	2 / 10	Ensure better the impact — 4 / 32	127
Schedule Management	No impact or need	Need better Mgt of Contact Labor — 0 / 0	Need better timing of tasks — 10 / 100	Minor — 6 / 36	No needs — 1 / 7	Work on scheduling — 0 / 0	5 / 25	No impact or needs — 0 / 0	168
Software Distribution Management	Transparent	No impact or Needs — 0 / 0	Could be automated — 0 / 0	No impact — 3 / 18	Better Notifications — 0 / 0	No impact — 3 / 27	0 / 0	No impact — 0 / 0	27

Figure 5.6 Process Selection Worksheet

Consensus Approach

The consensus-based approach of process prioritization uses a set of open-ended questions to select the best processes for improvement. This approach recognizes that processes can be selected using a human perspective instead of a numerical score or ranking method. The consensus approach fits well in those companies not accustomed to formal or structured decision analysis tools.

Process selection is facilitated through one or more sessions attended by people from Information Systems, the process team, process participants, and business leaders. Perspectives of executives, managers, process owners, and the participants are an important part of process selection. The open-ended questions are designed to cultivate participant views, as well as emotions, concerning where process work needs to be done. Initially, this approach may be difficult because it relies extensively on the articulation and interpersonal skills of the participants and facilitator. The facilitator also needs to limit the politics, egos, and criticism among the participants. When managed correctly, the consensus session will result in a broader understanding of the issues and a deeper understanding of the drivers for process change.

It is important in the consensus session not to try to deeply interrogate every process. The amount of time this will take is great and it does not add significant value. Therefore, the questions are organized into two sets: one to NARROW the processes down to the most important at this time and a second to EXPLORE in more detail the opportunities of each process. The consensus discussion first asks a set of four narrowing questions for every process:

- Is the business being impacted by weaknesses in the process?
- Do those who work in the process feel significant pain from the process?
- Do the customers of the process desire a change?
- Is the time right to address this process?

Once the number of processes has been narrowed, each remaining one is explored further in order to select the best process for improvement with exploratory questions:

- What is the customer feedback which suggest that the process should be improved?
- What are the desired outcomes of choosing this process?
- What kind of visibility will the process improvement provide?
- What are the risks of waiting to improve this process?

The consensus approach is effective because it recognizes the value of discussion and interchange in the decision-making process. There may be other questions more appropriate to a particular organization. These may include:

- Do user demands require immediate action?
- Does the process need to be improved to meet headcount requirements?
- Does the process need to be improved to meet budget requirements?
- Will success of the process be at risk without improvements?
- Will the image of Information Systems be impacted without improvements?
- What is the risk associated with the process?
- Are process improvements required for other projects?

We should not underestimate the ability of individuals, especially those involved in the process, to agree on issues and concerns. The challenge in this approach is documenting the perspectives of those participating. As time passes, having a record of the consensus will help the group to stay on track when scrutiny and questions begin.

Opportunity Approach

The opportunity approach recognizes that improvement depends on the current state of the process. The current state of the process is often referred to as its maturity or capability. Is the process doing everything it needs to do? Is it capable? Is it meeting the customers' needs? Has it developed and matured? There are several indicators that determine if a process is mature.

- The process has defined *flows* of information, people, or items.
- The process is *effective* in meeting customer requirements.
- The process is *efficient* in utilizing resources and time.
- The process is managed with appropriate *costs*.

Specific questions that determine how mature a process is include:

- Does a standard process exist?
- Is the process accurately documented?
- Are procedures in place to sufficiently support the process?
- Are appropriate tools used and integrated where necessary to automate the process?
- Is the process proactive in nature?

- Are metrics published that measure the effectiveness and efficiency of the process?
- Are service level agreements or target metrics in place for the process?
- Is customer feedback obtained from the process?
- Is the process continuously improved?
- Does formal training exist for the process?
- Is there a single process owner responsible for the process end to end?
- Does the process cross organizational boundaries if necessary?
- Are roles and responsibilities clearly defined for those involved in the process?

The more questions that are answered with *yes*, the more mature the process already is, and the less opportunity there is for process improvement. A more detailed list of questions to grade each process can be found in Appendix A.

Like the value analysis described earlier, the opportunity for improvement can be described in several levels.

- **Low opportunity:** The process is mature and is managed in a sufficient manner related to the characteristics of flow, effectiveness, efficiency, and cost.
- **Medium opportunity:** The process has elements or signs of flow, effectiveness, efficiency, or cost management to some degree but is not yet at a desired point.
- **High opportunity:** The process lacks many components that would make it perform as desired, including characteristics of flow, effectiveness, efficiency, and cost.

These three ratings provide a means of categorizing the opportunities of process improvement. As an example, let us describe a Performance and Availability Management Process that has not yet been invested in or improved. There are no metrics and no improvement cycles. Given our definitions above, the improvement opportunity would be high. The process is not doing everything it needs to; it is not capable; and it is not meeting the needs of the organization.

At this point, there is a choice of whether to take action based solely on opportunity, to combine with the consensus approach, or to compare the improvement opportunities with the business value discussed earlier. With this approach, it is clear that the critical processes are those that are high in value and high in improvement opportunities. These are the processes that should be addressed first. Likewise, processes that are not of high value and appear to be functioning well should not be selected for improvement efforts. Figure 5.7 shows a matrix that may

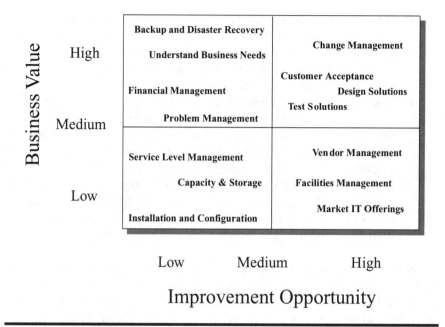

Figure 5.7 Opportunity Grid

be used to organize process initiatives. Each process should be placed into the area based on ratings of business value and improvement opportunity.

Of the five approaches discussed, the opportunity approach offers a balance between the criteria approach, which is analytically driven, and the consensus approach, which is subjectively driven. It provides structure and indicates specific direction for process improvement.

Metric Approach

This approach recognizes that measurement data on existing processes can be used to select which process to improve. As discussed in Chapter 3, metrics are critical to a successful Information Systems organization. Metrics are also the foundation of continuous improvement. When a metric frequently drifts out of the desired range of performance, it is an indication that the process is not capable and there is a need to select a process for improvement. Processes that are measured within Information Systems are typically well defined and mature. Therefore, this approach is best suited for environments that have mature processes and simply need guidance on which processes to improve next.

When considering the metrics approach to select processes, there are several questions to keep in mind.

- **What is, or was, the original intent of the measure?** Chances are that the original intent of the measure was to monitor, adjust, or guide the process. In order to prevent a poor decision, consider the original intent of the measure and make sure that it is a good indicator for improvement.
- **Does the data being gathered correctly represent the process?** We must be careful not to let a single measure distort the view of a process. We need to question whether the measure is indeed the best to use in making a process decision. Often it may be necessary to use several measures to determine the state of a particular process.
- **Is the system that gathers the metrics ongoing and accurate?** Timeliness of measurement data is always important. Nothing will cloud the selection of a process or improvement effort more quickly than using the metric approach with outdated data.

With this understanding of how and why the measures were established, we proceed with using the data to make a process selection decision. The decision logic is based on two factors: where the process is today and where it needs to be in the future. For mature processes, the metrics approach is one of the best methods to select a process for improvement. Identifying the process, understanding the current measure, and establishing a future target are all elements that can combine to select which process to improve next.

Evolution Approach

The evolution approach recognizes that processes can be prioritized based on the process evolution. As outlined in Chapter 1, there are five stages of process evolution: Firefighting, Desire, Beginning, Proactive, and World Class. With this approach, the order of working on processes is aligned to the current position of the company on the process evolution continuum. If, for example, a company is at the Beginning stage, it should focus on infrastructure processes such as Security Management Process or Schedule Management Process. On the contrary, if a company is at the World Class stage, focus will be on the mature processes such as Information Systems Strategic Planning Process or Customer Satisfaction Process. The evolution approach is designed to match the process improvement work to the level of evolution of the company.

Figure 5.8 demonstrates the alignment of information system processes to the five stages of the evolution. Notice how this approach aligns many of the system and application processes to the early stages of evolution and many of the relationship and resource processes to the later stages. The evolution approach recognizes that each stage is defined by the

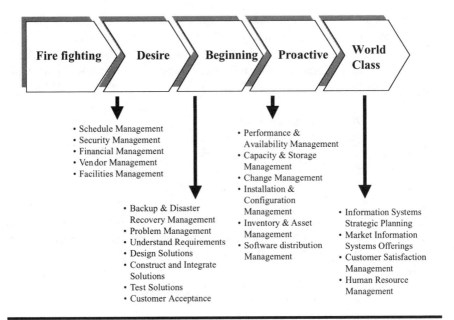

Figure 5.8 Evolution Approach

presence of a specific set of processes. To use this approach, we simply identify where on the evolution continuum an organization is and reference the set of processes that should be in place at this stage. If the organization is missing some of these key processes, then we have narrowed the choice and should begin by putting these missing processes in place. Before beginning, we review the processes associated with other stages of the evolution and determine what gaps there may be in the organization. We need to watch for processes that may not exist or be formally defined in the organization. If these processes are downstream on the evolution, we must consider adjusting the perspective of where the organization is on the continuum and use this as motivation to begin establishing or improving those processes.

The alignment of each process to a specific stage of the evolution may need to be adjusted for a particular organization. Culture barriers, environmental factors, and even resource constraints all play a role in how processes are aligned to each stage of the process evolution.

SELECT PROCESSES

Once the prioritization process is complete, the selection is relatively simple. The more complex question becomes how many processes the company should work on at the same time. Perhaps only one, the top-priority process, or perhaps several. Some companies prefer to have several process improvement teams to demonstrate progress and improve quickly in needed areas. Such programs can be daunting and lead to neglect of the normal business. Consider the following when determining how many processes to tackle:

- The amount of available resources
- The urgency of necessary changes
- The potential cost and budget constraints
- The amount of change the organization can absorb
- The skill set of the resources available

With the selection process complete, it is now time to begin the exciting part of information systems process improvement, the mapping of the current state, and the design of a new and improved process.

PITFALLS TO AVOID

Following are pitfalls to avoid when selecting processes:

- **Selection of pet processes:** As with any prioritization effort, if those involved in selecting the process already have a direction in mind for process improvement, they will probably position facts to favor their direction. We need to watch for this tendency and use a structured approach such as those outlined in this chapter to get to the facts and objectively prioritize the processes.
- **Thinking every process is important:** Selection methods should demonstrate a balanced perspective of the work that needs to be done. Rating every process as important does not demonstrate an effective selection technique. We must work toward what is important to the organization.
- **Not using facts in the selection process:** One of the biggest challenges in selecting a process is to use facts rather than perceptions. Facts take time to gather. It is important to spend that time. It is better to extend the time of the selection process than end up working on a process that does not have an impact to the operation of Information Systems.

KEY POINTS TO REMEMBER

■ Information system processes offer value to the organization and support the financial, operational, and strategic direction of the business.
■ Prioritizing processes is essential. It channels resources and improvements toward the most valuable processes for the business.
■ There are many different approaches to prioritizing and selecting processes. An approach should be chosen that matches the management style and company environment.
■ The number of process improvement projects at any one time will vary depending on the environment.
■ Deliverables for the third step, Process Selection, include:
  ■ Process selection worksheet
  ■ Prioritized processes

NOTES AND IDEAS FOR MY PROCESS IMPROVEMENT EFFORT

6

CURRENT STATE PROCESS ASSESSMENT

"The important thing is not to stop questioning."

Einstein

Now it's starting to get exciting. Processes have been identified, prioritized, and selected for improvement. The next step (Step 4) of the process methodology is to perform a current state process assessment. Following are the tasks for this step:

- **Gather Information:** Gather information about the current process.
  Conducting interviews
  - Observing the process
  - Performing the process
- **Flowchart:** Flowchart the current process to obtain understanding.
  Map processes across departments
  - Cross-functional flowcharting
  - Steps to create cross-functional flowchart
  - Hints for creating the cross-functional flowchart
- **Analyze Flowchart:** Analyze the flowchart created.
  Flowchart characteristics

These tasks are depicted in Figure 6.1 and described below.

Process Improvement Methodology

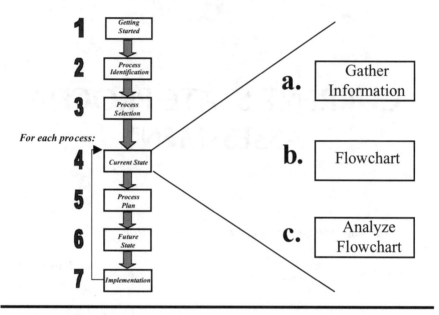

Figure 6.1 Current State Process Assessment

GATHER INFORMATION

The current state process assessment begins by gathering information. The ability to gather information will be critical to the success of improving information systems processes. The purpose of gathering information is to provide the data necessary to make process improvements. There are three approaches that can be used to gather information.

Conducting Interviews

Interviews should be held with process participants and customers to obtain details of events and the flow within a process. Interviews are the most effective method of gathering large amounts of information. Selecting the appropriate participants is important. The following are characteristics to consider when selecting interview candidates.

- Length of service in the process
- Detailed working knowledge of the process
- Leadership position in the process

Schedule the interviews in advance and provide the candidate with an appropriate number of background details. These background details may include:

- Why the interview is being conducted
- Who is working on this project
- Who in management is supporting these efforts
- How and why the candidate was selected to participate in the interview
- Length of time needed for the interview
- What types of questions will be asked
- How the results will be used

It is best to hold interviews away from the work area. This helps create a comfortable, nonthreatening environment, free of interruptions. The interview session itself will vary in length depending on the process being studied and the role the interviewee has in the process. A general rule of thumb is that no one interview should last longer than 60 to 90 minutes. If more time is required, multiple sessions should be scheduled.

When the interview begins, the background as to why the person was selected and all other relevant information should be reviewed to ensure the interviewee understands the intent. With that accomplished, the interview questioning can begin. Following are the typical interview questions for process improvement that should be covered:

- What process activities do you perform?
- What are the steps of your process?
- How do you know your process steps are effective?
- What are the required inputs to your process?
- Who are your customers?
- What are your customers' requirements?
- What feedback do you receive?
- What process measures do you have?
- What are your quality issues?
- What are your process issues?
- What would you change in the process if you could?
- What would happen if you didn't do this process?

During the interview, there will undoubtedly be a need to explore and clarify answers on various topics. It is important to recognize that the interviewees may not clearly describe their work. Often, interviewees unintentionally omit information from their responses. They may not specify something clearly, or they may imply something is happening, when they really may not know.

•Select appropriate participants

•Provide background and understanding

•Schedule interview time and location

•Hold interview session

•Organize information

Figure 6.2 Aspects of Interviewing

When the interviewee begins to quantify something in general terms such as *never* or *always* or *somebody*, questions should be asked that clarify these generalizations. Processes are dynamic, and generalizations will cause difficulty in designing improvements. Recognizing this type of response and adding follow-up questions is a skill that is developed through interviewing experience.

As process information is gathered, information about the customers who receive outputs from the process and the suppliers who provide inputs to the process is also needed. Gathering this type of information will require face-to-face interviews with both suppliers and customers.

Your next interviews should be with the customers of the process. Their opinions on the current process should be obtained. What they want to receive in terms of services or products is critical to the redesign of the process. Customer requirements need to be identified and described in specific terms. Descriptions such as *accurate* or *timely* do not provide specific enough descriptions. Good customer requirements are defined with numbers. The impact of emerging information technologies must also be considered. For example, when designing the new process, the need to consider the impact of e-business on the process should be kept in mind. After interviews with the customers are completed, the suppliers should be interviewed.

Some of the answers to the questions may not be available. People can have a difficult time detailing what they provide or receive from a process. They also have a difficult time expressing what requirements they have. Therefore, it is essential to guide both suppliers and customers and not get frustrated. There are many aspects to interviewing and, as shown in Figure 6.2, all of these aspects are needed to create a productive interview.

Observing the Process

Ideally, after the interview, both the interviewer and the interviewee should go to the work area and observe the activity discussed in the interview.

If this is not immediately possible, a time should be arranged to observe the process firsthand. Perceptions of the process may change substantially after gathering information from the interview. During the interview, participants will describe what they believe happens in the process. Observing the process firsthand identifies reality. Are requests prioritized as outlined? Where is the Problem Management Process working? Is the Installation and Configuration Management Process really keeping applications up to date? These are simple examples to consider when observing a process. There are several techniques used to observe the process and document the findings:

- Further questioning
- Note taking
- Sketching

Observation of key process metrics will assist in the data gathering stage. Observing the process will stimulate additional questions, but if given the opportunity, one should try performing or participating in the process to solidify understanding.

Performing the Process

The technique of gathering information through direct participation creates deep and lasting knowledge. Actually working in the process provides better insight into what is important and what is not. This means performing some of the work. Maybe it will be answering calls at the Help Desk, staying late to perform backups, or assigning asset tags to incoming equipment. Performing a process will spawn new ideas, increase respectability, and ease the fears of those who will be affected by any change in the process.

FLOWCHART THE PROCESS

Now that all of the information has been gathered, a process flowchart can be created. A flowchart or process map is a picture of how work is accomplished in a process. It shows the activities, flow, and output of a process much in the same manner that a road map shows how to get from Point A to Point B. It combines symbols, lines, and words and shows them in a manner that demonstrates the current state of the process. The flowcharting process uses symbols to communicate the type of activity being performed. With a road map, being familiar with each symbol helps us interpret and make decisions on where we are going. The same is true in flowcharting. The most commonly used symbols are shown in Figure 6.3.

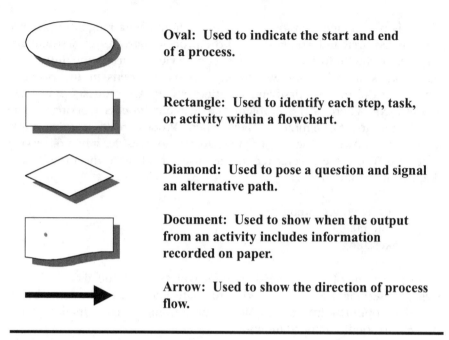

Oval: Used to indicate the start and end of a process.

Rectangle: Used to identify each step, task, or activity within a flowchart.

Diamond: Used to pose a question and signal an alternative path.

Document: Used to show when the output from an activity includes information recorded on paper.

Arrow: Used to show the direction of process flow.

Figure 6.3 Flowcharting Symbols

Map Processes across Departments

Once a process is mapped onto a flowchart, it can be reviewed as to how the process cuts across multiple departments (see Figure 6.4).

Often, departments establish boundaries that make the process more difficult. How does this happen?

- **Departments are familiar to people; processes usually are not.** Many of us work in companies where we are part of a department. The department contains people that share similar work and objectives. Unfortunately, processes are not as easy to see as these people. Processes exist within departments, hidden from easy association to the people that support them.
- **Departments are documented on charts; processes usually are not.** The focus on departments leads companies to document departments on organizational charts. Processes, however, are seldom documented and used to align the overall business of the company.
- **Departments have names; processes usually do not.** Whether it is Data Processing or Online Services, companies identify departments by names. This provides clarity and association by those doing the work. Processes often do not have names associated with them. This makes identifying with processes more difficult.

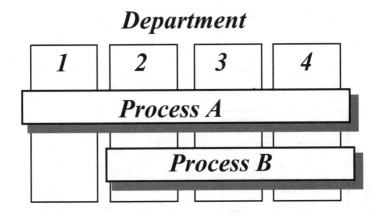

Figure 6.4 Cross-Departmental Model

■ **People are put in charge of departments not processes.** Managers, supervisors, and team leaders all help combine people, materials, and information to get work completed in a process. However, organizations still tend to put people in charge of departments not processes.

Cross-Functional Flowcharting

Although companies organize themselves by departments, most of the processes flow across departments. A cross-functional flowchart is a very effective tool to map the current work processes in this environment. Besides identifying all of the departments or persons participating in the process, the cross-functional flowchart allows for a visual analysis of workflow between and among departments. This analysis is important because each time work crosses functions there are potential exposures for waste, bottlenecks, or miscommunication.

The distinguishing characteristic of a cross-functional flowchart is that it identifies the departments or people that perform various steps of the process. These departments or people are known as functions and are organized as separate vertical columns on the chart. Under each function, the associated process steps are identified. Figure 6.5 shows a traditional flowchart for a portion of the Inventory and Asset Management Process. Notice the linear nature of the flow. Although the steps are clearly described, the chart does not provide a view of who is involved in the process.

Figure 6.6 demonstrates the clarity and understanding of a cross-functional flowchart for the same process. Notice the clarity of who is

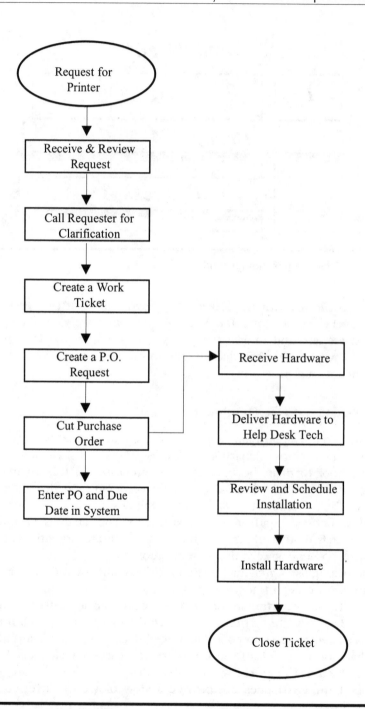

Figure 6.5 Traditional Flowchart

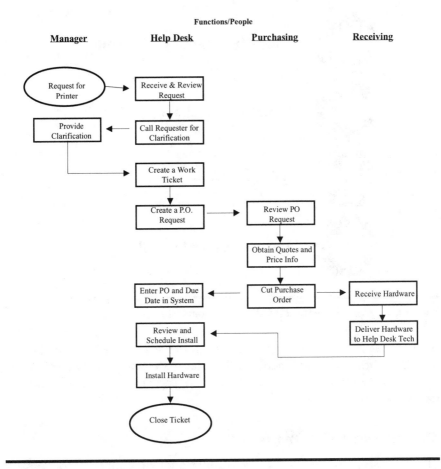

Figure 6.6 Cross-Functional Flowchart

doing what as well as the pattern of the process flow. This encompassing view is the most effective way to understand the current process. It will also be the most effective view of the new and improved process.

Steps to Create the Cross-Functional Flowchart

There are four basic steps to create a cross-functional flowchart as shown in Figure 6.7. First, identify the departments or people that participate in the process. The more specific as to who performs the task, the more clarity there will be concerning what actually goes on in the process. Second, flowchart the process. As outlined above, charting demonstrates the process flow by combining symbols, lines, and words. Third, attach

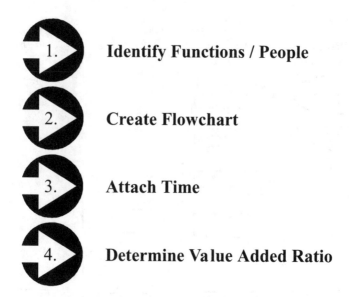

Figure 6.7 Steps to Create the Cross-Functional Flowchart

time. The cycle time of a process defines much of its efficiency. The last step in creating a cross-functional flowchart is to calculate the efficiency of the process through a value added ratio. Each of these steps is further explained below.

Identify Departments/People

The first step in creating a cross-functional flowchart is to identify the departments or people that participate in the process. For certain processes it may be more effective to list the departments involved, such as Human Resources, Accounting, or Help Desk. For other processes it will be more effective to list the specific people involved. This may be done by position, such as Manager, Requester, or Technician, or by the actual name of each person involved in the process. The more specific we can be in defining who participates in the process, the more clarity there will be on the activities or steps being performed. Once the functions or people are identified, they should be listed across the top of the cross-functional flowchart by order as they appear in the process. The intent is to identify every department or person involved in the process. However, remaining flexible is important. The team members may not realize every function or person involved in the process until they have begun flowcharting.

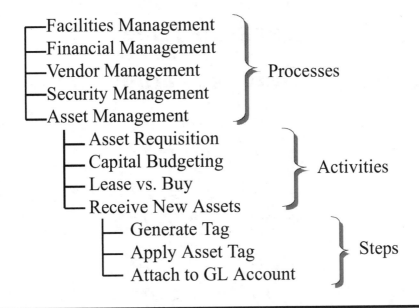

Figure 6.8 Process Level Example

Create Flowchart

One of the biggest challenges in developing a current state process map is determining the level of detail to flowchart the process. For example, at the highest level consider a *process*, called Inventory and Asset Management. This would include many *activities*, one of which would be to receive new assets. Receiving new assets includes many *steps* such as generate tag, apply asset tag, and attach to an account number. There are many steps which make up receiving new assets, and many other activities such as asset requisition that make up the entire process of Inventory and Asset Management. Again, processes are made up of activities, and activities are made up of steps. It is important that the cross-functional flowchart remain at the same level during the current state mapping. In other words, we do not create a flowchart that includes both activities and steps. Staying at the same level will assist in collecting data and analyzing the results. Figure 6.8 depicts these three levels and shows related examples.

As a rule of thumb, the cross-functional flowchart is completed at the activity level for every process. The steps that make up these activities are generally detailed in a procedure or work instruction, not on the cross-functional flowchart. For example, the activity of entering a problem call into the call tracker software consists of many steps, one being "Enter account information in business name field and hit return." The detail

Back-up Time

Date	Time
8/21	2:53
8/24	3:14
8/25	2:45
8/26	2:54
8/27	3:02
8/28	2:46

Figure 6.9 Log Example

represented by this step is best communicated in a procedure or work instruction, not on a flowchart.

Another consideration when charting a process is whether to include decision boxes. Decision boxes are best used when a process has multiple paths and the choosing requires a decision. A decision box is actually a diamond-shaped box filled with text, which identifies the point in the process at which a decision must be made. The subsequent activities or steps will vary based on this decision. For example, "If the hardware request is under $5,000, it can bypass a manager's approval. If it is more than $5,000, it will require approval." Typically a decision box is driven by a YES-NO decision. The need to chart decision boxes is simply a matter of multiple paths, speed, and clarity. Time spent detailing every question and process decision may slow the team down. At first, it may be more effective to not include decision boxes and simply show multiple paths (arrows) extending from a single task. As the flow is solidified, the decision boxes can be added later to provide clarity. This will help the charting exercise move along quickly and provide the most useful results for the process improvement or reengineering initiative.

Ticket Traveler #_245_

Steps	Date	Tech
Receive Request	9/21	TV
Order Hardware	9/21	TV
Received Hardware	9/23	KO
Configured and Installed	9/24	KO
Closed Ticket	9/24	KO

Figure 6.10 Traveler Example

Attach Time

Every process has a beginning and an end. The time that it takes to travel through the process from beginning to end is known as *cycle time*. Cycle time is a critical measure that indicates the speed, responsiveness, and efficiency of a process. It is important when doing the current state cross-functional flowchart to understand the cycle time of the process and how to calculate and analyze it to improve the process. There are several techniques for collecting time data in a process. A combination of these techniques may actually be needed to create a total understanding for how long a specific process takes.

- **Timepieces:** Timepieces are best suited for repetitive, shorter length cycles where the time is less than ten minutes. Timepieces are often used when a micro view of the process is needed or when many steps need to be timed.
- **Logs:** Logs are best suited for longer cycles greater than ten minutes. Logs remain stationary. The work activity moves past the log and data is recorded. An example is shown in Figure 6.9.
- **Travelers:** Travelers are best suited for longer cycles. As the name implies, travelers "travel" with the work through the process. Each step needs to be predetermined and created as a blank on the traveler slip. The blanks are then dated, timed, and often initialed throughout the flow. Travelers are most effective on a temporary basis. An example of a traveler is shown in Figure 6.10.
- **Date Fields:** Often the dates or date fields on a form or computer screen can be used as a basis for time data collection. Computer fields and time stamps are the most accurate methods of capturing time data.

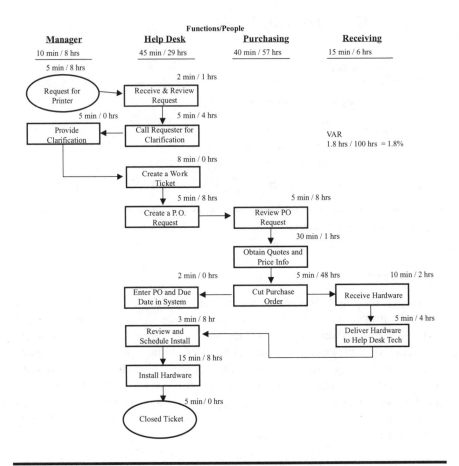

Figure 6.11 Cross-Functional Flowchart with Time Data

■ **Calculated Time:** Sometimes the value added time for a task varies. This may be due to volume or processing differences. For example, Help Desk tickets for break-fix issues can be handled in approximately 10 minutes. Tickets for new system configurations take roughly 20 minutes. The real average of these is not 15. When you study a process, you need to consider the volume of process activity. Let us say that 75 percent of people get software installations and 25 percent get new systems. The weighted average shows a more realistic number for how long tickets take: (75 × 10) + (25 × 20) / 100 = 12.5 minutes. Again, this is often referred to as a weighted average time. When it is preferable to evaluate the average time of a process step in weighted context, this needs to be considered.

■ **Interview Data:** Although often least factual, there are certain times when obtaining an indication for the length of the process through an interview is appropriate. This may occur in cases of very quick cycles or low value added in comparison with the time required. It may also be effective in less frequent or distant processes that cannot be observed personally. Data based on facts comes closer to the real target.

Once the time data is collected, it can be summarized and attached to the cross-functional flowchart. Figure 6.11 demonstrates how time data is attached to the cross-functional flowchart. Both work time and total cycle time are noted on the chart. A step noted as '5 min / 8 hrs' means that each time the step is performed it takes an average of 5 minutes and until the next person takes it, over 8 hours usually passes. Notice how the process time is listed with each step and the sum of all steps within a given function is summarized at the top. This provides the viewer a perspective for how much time a specific function spends performing the process.

Determine Value Added Ratio

As mentioned earlier, cycle time is the time to travel through the process from beginning to end. Ideally, all of this time would be made up of work being done in the process and no time would be wasted. Realistically, that is hard to achieve. Often processes contain wastes of delay, quality errors, and even movement. The portion of cycle time that is waste is called *non-value added time*. The portion of cycle time that is work is called *value added time*. Every process must maximize the process work and minimize the process waste. A useful measure for how well this is being achieved is known as the *Value Added Ratio* (VAR). Value Added Ratio is the proportion of work compared with waste in a process. The greater the value added ratio, the more efficient the process is. The value added ratio calculation for the Purchasing function in Figure 6.11 can be found below in Figure 6.12.

The ideal value added ratio is 100 percent as this would indicate all work and no waste. The closer a process is to this ideal number, the better its efficiency. Granted, 100 percent is rather theoretical. Most processes have value added ratios that range from 1 percent to 10 percent. A ratio of 25 percent is often quoted as world class. This is due to the natural prevalence of waste in processes. Times spent waiting, moving, checking, and redoing are significant parts of many processes. Most of these wasted steps go unnoticed. People adjust work patterns, shift themselves between processes, and sometimes even mistake waste as actual

$$\frac{\text{Work}}{\text{Work} + \text{Waste}} \quad \text{X} \quad 100\%$$

$$\frac{\text{40 Minutes}}{\text{40 min} + \text{57 Hrs}} \quad \text{X} \quad 100\%$$

$$= .011 \quad \text{X} \quad 100\%$$

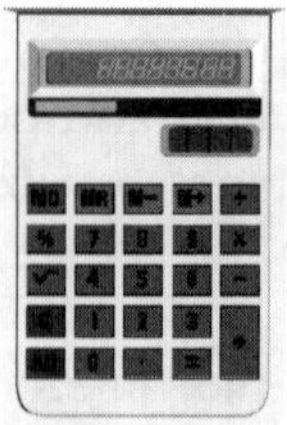

$$\frac{\text{Value Added Ratio}}{\text{for Purchasing}} = 1.1\%$$

Figure 6.12 Calculating Value Added Ratio

work. During current state process mapping, waste should be identified within the process. It should be flagged and charted. One of the main goals of the improvement or reengineering effort will be to reduce process waste. Since waste is so prevalent, spend time working first to reduce the waste, not the work. This is the easiest way to improve a processes value added ratio.

Hints for Creating the Cross-Functional Flowchart

There are several hints that will make cross-functional flowcharting successful.

- **Start with sticky notes.** Try to resist the temptation to draft the flowchart on paper. So save erasing and repositioning steps, use sticky notes on a wall as a starting method.
- **Don't draw lines.** With an understanding that new steps and new paths will be identified, refrain from initially drawing lines that commit to a flow. Picture the flow lines and solidify them in writing only near the end of the charting process.
- **Do the flowcharting with groups of people.** Very few people know all of the steps of every process. Bringing together the process participants and sharing a variety of perspectives will increase the success of the outcome.
- **Keep decision boxes out.** Decision boxes usually are answered yes or no. To simplify the initial charting, picture them on the chart, and add them later for clarity and understanding.

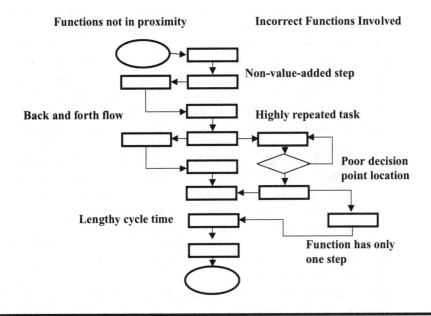

Figure 6.13 Cross-Functional Flowchart Analysis Points

- **Don't get distracted by computer programs.** There is a time and place to use technology to chart processes, but it is not always right away. Stay with the sticky notes or other simple tools before turning on the computer and creating a clean and neat-looking chart.
- **Follow a charting process.** Creating the "as is" cross-functional flowchart is most successful if a few steps are done in a specific order. Follow the steps to create the cross-functional flowchart.

ANALYZE THE FLOWCHART

The current state process assessment ends with the analysis of the cross-functional flowchart. It may not be evident at first, but there is a vast amount of information and data contained in a cross-functional flowchart. The analysis of this information and data is critical for understanding the current process and formulating the process objectives. So how do we do the analysis? What should we look for? What characteristics are important to evaluate? Following are analysis points to consider when reviewing a cross-functional flowchart and indicate improvements that should be made. Figure 6.13 demonstrates these points.

- **Are there back-and-forth flows?** One of the most common characteristics of poor process flow is the tendency to bounce back and forth between one person or function and another. On the cross-functional flowchart, this flow is characterized by back-and-forth lines continuously crossing functional boundaries. These back-and-forth flows are often a result of processes that naturally flow between functions, responsibilities that are often not aligned, and the need for checks and approvals that exists in many corporate processes. To address back-and-forth flows it is necessary to redefine work responsibilities, integrate tasks under the same function or person, and blend or eliminate activities altogether.

■ **Are there functions with only one activity or step?** Another characteristic of a poor process is when one person or function does only one single activity or step. Such a situation often occurs when only one person has the needed expertise or equipment to perform a step or when the step is associated with an approval. Solutions to persons or functions that have only one step involve training individuals with more involvement in the process to take on the single step activity, validate the need for approvals and authorizations, and reposition equipment and assets underneath functions with greater roles in the process. As with back-and-forth flows, eliminating single activity functions will help streamline the process and prevent delay.

■ **Are there highly repeated tasks?** During process analysis, highly repeated tasks are a sign that the process needs to change. On the cross-functional flowchart, this is evident through flows that double back and repeat. The sources of these repeated tasks are often quality issues that require steps of the process to be redone or additional information and work that is needed each time throughout the step. To address highly repeated tasks, it is necessary to modify the job function, step, or process and eliminate the need for repetition.

■ **Are there activities or steps not in proximity?** It should come as to no surprise that, when people or functions are in physical proximity with each other, they relate in a more effective and efficient manner. This is not immediately evident on the cross-functional flowchart unless the proximity between functions is questioned. Often the constraints of buildings and surroundings, the location of people participating in the process, or the dependency on stationary equipment prevent the process steps from being performed in proximity. To address proximity issues, it is important to move people or functions involved in a process closer together, shift activities and steps to another function, or reposition the hardware or physical constraints of the process.

■ **Are decisions being made at the inappropriate time or place?** Although it may appear that decisions are being made throughout the entire process, in reality, there are usually a few critical decision points within a process. On the cross-functional flowchart, it is important to locate those decision points and ensure that the decisions are being made at the appropriate time or place. The decisions often change a process flow or address a specific requirement. During analysis the need for each decision and who should be making that decision should be considered.

■ **Are there lengthy cycle times?** The analysis of a cross-functional flowchart would not be complete without consideration of the process cycle time. Remember that cycle time indicates the total time it takes to deliver output to the customer. Process delay, excessive steps, or a lack of a cycle time focus and measurement can cause a lengthy cycle time. On the cross-functional flowchart lengthy cycle times become evident when time data is added. To improve this performance, it is necessary to reduce or eliminate wait times either before or after each step or activity, shorten the process, have a defined start and stop, and implement a measure that demonstrates the importance of cycle time.

■ **Are there non-value-added steps that can be eliminated or minimized?** It is important to understand that the analysis and focus of the process improvement effort needs to concentrate on the wasted activities and steps, and not the work. Wasted steps (such as delays, transportation problems, and quality errors) may not be readily evident on the flowchart if only the value-added activities were charted. During the analysis of the flowchart, non-value-added steps should be identified. Eliminating these from the process will lead to increased process performance.

■ **Are the correct functions involved in the process?** Processes often evolve over time, and the people or functions involved in the process may no longer be necessary. In the analysis of the flowchart, it is important to question who or what functions are involved in the process. Are they still needed? How can the functions involved be streamlined? Questions should be posed that challenge what functions or people are involved.

PITFALLS TO AVOID

Following are pitfalls to avoid when mapping the current state process.

■ **Charting the incorrect level of the process:** It is important to work to keep the process map at the same level and not mix activities and steps on the same chart. The process should be flowcharted at the activity level. Further detail and specifics on each process step should be outlined in a procedural or work instruction document.

■ **Collection bias:** The methods and techniques for data collection must be objective. It is easy to get distracted and chase data that does not relate to the process being studied. If possible, process work should be assigned to people who are not involved in the process on a day-to-day basis. Through this technique and simple awareness it is possible to overcome any collection bias.

■ **Not accounting for variability:** Process steps are often variable and this variability needs to be accounted for in mapping the process. Time is the most common process variable, but other variables include the quality and relevancy of the step. As the process is mapped, it is important to consider the effects of process variability on the outcome and, if substantial, document the variation and consider it during process redesign.

■ **Process paralysis:** Everything we do can be made into a process. Every call, every interaction, every move can be forced into some process. It is this overbearing process perspective that often creates process paralysis. Everything happening in Information Systems does not need to be charted, mapped, or documented. It is necessary to identify the critical outputs from the Information System activities, follow those outputs back to activities that produced them, then tie those activities together into key processes. This approach will help avoid getting process paralysis.

■ **Differing process perspectives:** While working on process mapping, it is important to be aware that others may view the steps of a process differently. These differing views are often rooted in experience, ownership, and beliefs of what actually happens. Involving a cross-section of participants in mapping the cross-functional process will eliminate many of the issues associated with differing perspectives.

■ **Not thinking outside the box:** There are many points to consider during process analysis. Most of these points address aspects of the process flow. It is also important to ensure the right mind set in those analyzing the process. It is not uncommon to have participants in the process involved in analyzing the process. It is necessary to work with these individuals to balance their own perspectives and experiences with those of fresh ideas.

KEY POINTS TO REMEMBER

■ Process information can be gathered through interviews, observing, or actually participating in the process.

- Cross-functional flowcharting is used to map the activities and steps of a process.
- Time data can be attached to the cross-functional flowchart and a value-added ratio calculated to quantify the efficiency of the process.
- Analyzing the cross-functional flowchart creates an understanding of the current process and helps formulate the objectives for the improved process.
- Deliverables from step four, Current State Process Assessment, include:
  - Interview and observation notes
  - Cross-functional flowchart with time
  - Cross-functional flowchart analysis

NOTES AND IDEAS FOR MY PROCESS IMPROVEMENT EFFORT

7

PROCESS PLAN

"Dare mighty things, even though checkered with failure, rather than to rank with those gray souls that know neither victory or defeat."

Theodore Roosevelt

It is now time to plan the new process. During this step, we will determine the process objectives, determine the metrics and baseline data, obtain benchmark information, and complete the process plan. Following are the tasks in this step:

- **Determine Process Objectives:** Define goals of the new process.
- **Determine Process Metrics:** Define the measures of the new process.
  - Efficiency and Effectiveness
  - Attribute Data and Variable Data
- **Obtain Baseline Data:** Obtain baseline data for current measure
- **Benchmark the Process:** Obtain industry data
- **Develop Process Plan:** Develop the process plan that will guide the process change.
  - Process Team
  - Case for Action
  - Process Tasks

These tasks are shown in Figure 7.1.

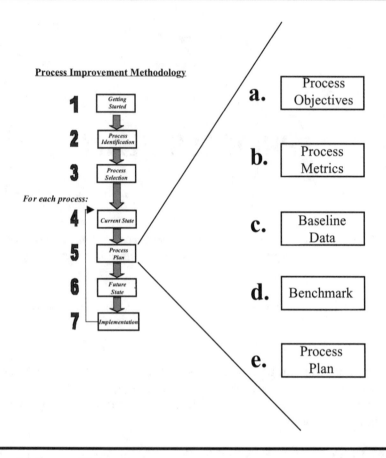

Figure 7.1 Process Plan

DETERMINE PROCESS OBJECTIVES

Through the analysis of the current process, a vision can be created for what the process is to become. What must be improved? What is the goal of the process improvement effort? What are the process objectives? Establishing these objectives is critical to the process effort. By this point the project participants now have a solid understanding of the complete process. The process has been identified and selected for change, the participants have been interviewed, and the current state of the process has been flowcharted and analyzed. Now this information can be used to finalize the objectives of the new process.

It is difficult to identify a set of boilerplate objectives for each process within Information Systems. The culture of the organization, the styles of those within the Information Systems group, and the process work needing to be accomplished are all considerations in setting objectives. Appendix A offers guidance in setting objectives by listing a set of components that

Figure 7.2 Characteristics of Process Goals

are critical for success of each information system process. Again, it is important to use these as a guide and adjust the objectives to one's organization accordingly.

Objectives are detailed in terms of goals that describe the desired outcome from the process initiative. For example, "reduce the cycle time of the hardware request process to four hours" is an objective goal; "improve the satisfaction of installations" is a subjective goal. Both types of goals have their value in the planning process and throughout the project plan. As shown in Figure 7.2, there are several characteristics that the process goals should have.

- **Measurable:** Key process goals need to be measurable. This ensures that gains are made and not lost. At the beginning of the process effort, measurable goals guide the project team in a direction. After the effort, measurable goals assist in controlling and correcting process performance. It is critical that measurable goals are established with both of these in mind.
- **Realistic:** Goals provide the targets that will determine the success of the process initiative. These goals should be realistic while still stretching the process and participants to be better. Creating goals that are not attainable will only dampen the spirits of the participants. Goals should be set that consider the time, skills, money, and resources available to the team.
- **Clear and Specific:** Process goals need to be clear and specific. Generalizations such as *improve, enhance,* and *change* are not effective unless narrowed in scope to the specific process being addressed. Clear goals are usually short in length and stated best

in one phrase. When an objective measure is integrated, the goal quickly becomes specific.

- **Mutually Understood:** The audience for process goals is broad. Team members, process participants, customers, managers, and suppliers all need to understand the process goals. These individuals need to have a stake in the goals as well. Therefore, it is important to choose goals that apply to many of the process stakeholders.

Objectives for the process improvement effort can be classified as two relatively straightforward types: *musts* (requirements) and *wants* (desires). Objectives classified as *musts*:

- *Must* be obtained to consider the process effort a success.
- Are measurable and quantifiable.
- Are clear and specific, understood by everyone involved.

Objectives classified as *wants*:

- Do not need to be accomplished to consider the process effort a success; however, being able to complete a *want* will further enhance the result of the process effort.
- Do not need to have a metric.
- May address the more subtle, softer elements of the process effort.

Objectives, when described in the *must* and *want* format outlined above, define the direction for the process improvement effort. With the most critical objectives being *musts*, and *musts* being measurable, it is important to understand how to use process metrics. Figure 7.3 demonstrates examples of *must* and *want* objectives.

DETERMINE PROCESS METRICS

As mentioned in Chapter 3, we are continually reacquainted with the old adage "you can't improve what you don't measure." In no other place is that statement more valid than in the area of process improvement. How is the process performing? Is it meeting the needs of its customers? Is it drifting away from the original intent? These questions and many others all ask for answers that can be found through good metrics. Yet, as often as we may hear such statements or recognize the value of good process metrics, the reality is that processes are seldom measured.

It is important to understand that process metrics are used for many different reasons. Metrics are used to

Problem Management Process Objectives

Musts

1) Improve resolution times to 75% within one hour.

2) Manage call volume to 1500 calls per month.

3) Improve time to answer with 95% in 30 seconds or less.

4) Reduce percentage of training type calls to <10%.

5) Meet monthly budget target of $123,000.

Wants

1) Begin using remote access software to resolve problems.

2) Improve the customer service attitude of technicians.

3) Respond to 85% of calls within one hour.

4) Establish service level agreements with 25% of departmens supported.

Figure 7.3 Examples of Process Objectives

- Monitor performance
- Set targets or goals
- Identify areas for improvement
- Indicate the achievement of targets or goals
- Show how effectively resources are used in the process
- Focus attention on important process characteristics
- Indicate areas for investigating and problem solving
- Indicate conditions that are out of control
- Allow priorities to be determined and set

Efficiency and Effectiveness

There are two major types of process metrics — efficiency and effectiveness. Each type is important to understand and integrate into the process being analyzed and changed. Figure 7.4 shows examples of efficiency and effectiveness metrics.

Efficiency is a measure of *how well the process delivers its output to its customers.* Efficiency measures are generally established for those involved in performing the process. In their simplest form, these measures answer the question:"Do we efficiently provide something our customers desire?"

Efficiency Metrics   Effectiveness Metrics

Efficiency Metrics	Effectiveness Metrics
Value added ratio	Accuracy
Percentage of utilization	Timeliness of response
Total wait time	Completeness of jobs
Total cycle time	Usefulness of solutions
Cost per unit processed	Consistency

Figure 7.4 Efficiency and Effectiveness Metrics

These measures provide an indication for how efficiently resources (such as people's time, costs, materials, and information) are consumed as the process transforms inputs to outputs. The fewer the resources consumed, the more efficient the process.

Effectiveness is a measure of *how well the output meets the needs of its customers.* Effectiveness measures are established not for the sake of those involved in the process but as a measure of customer needs and expectations. In their simplest form, these measures answer the question: "Do our customers receive desired results from our process?" These measures provide an indication for how effectively the needs and expectations of the customers are met.

Effectiveness measures are used to gauge the process's ability to meet the needs and expectations of its customers. As such, the customers need to be involved in establishing the most appropriate metrics. This is a challenge as customers generally have a difficult time articulating what they need from a process. Conditions such as *accurate* and *timely* are easy to express but difficult to ascertain. The following techniques are used to gather information on the types of metrics most appropriate.

- Customer interviews
- Surveys
- Complaints
- Focus groups

The goal for any of these techniques is to whittle down the metric possibilities to a few measures that are most likely to capture the effectiveness of the process.

Attribute Data and Variable Data

When measures are chosen to capture the efficiency and effectiveness of the process, data will be collected to support it. There are two types of

Attribute Measurements	Variable Measurements
Was the monthly performance below or above budget?	What percentage below or over budget was the month?
Was the back-up completed?	How many minutes did it take to complete back-ups?
Is there training for IS employees?	What are the annual training hours per IS employee?
Did the customer accept the program change?	What is the acceptance rate of new programs?

Figure 7.5 Attribute and Variable Measurements

data used to measure a process: attribute data and variable data. Examples of each are shown in Figure 7.5.

Attribute data are the types of data that are counted. The result will be simply a yes or no, pass or fail, up or down. The exact measurement does not matter, simply the occurrence of the event. Often attribute data are sufficient to make a determination of process performance.

Variable data are the types of data that are measured. The result will be a specific numeric value, or distribution of values, that indicates how the process is actually performing. Variable data is useful in making decisions involving many processes. The collection and summarization of variable data, although more complex and time-consuming than attribute data, yield results that provide a clear understanding of process performance. Chapter 3 references many types of variable metrics for Information Systems.

There are a few points worth mentioning about both attribute and variable metrics. These points will assist in understanding how to implement successful metrics to achieve process success.

- Metrics should be completed by the person(s) performing the process. This ensures timely feedback for correction or adjustment.
- Metrics should be completed in real time. Waiting to quantify or summarize performance will only move one farther from the reality that has just occurred.
- Metrics should be taken at critical points of the process. It is important to recognize that those critical points of the process may NOT be at the end of the process.
- When determining metrics, predicting what actions may be taken as a result of the measurement will help ensure that the metric is appropriate.

OBTAIN BASELINE DATA

With an understanding of efficiency and effectiveness, and the difference between attribute and variable data, baseline data on the current process can now be collected. Baseline data are collected on the existing process to

- Provide an understanding of the current process performance
- Help define the objectives of the new process effort
- Demonstrate the amount of gain and improvement of the future process

It is important to recognize that the existing processes may be lacking ideal measures and performance data. This is not uncommon. In fact, collecting baseline data is for the purpose of better understanding the current process performance. This presents a few challenges. As described in the previous section, measurements often require systems to collect data. These systems address

- How frequently data will be collected (e.g., hourly, daily, weekly)
- How it will be collected (e.g., automatically, manually)
- Format used to summarize the data (e.g., numbers, tables, charts, graphs)
- Method by which the information will be reviewed (e.g., individually, at staff meetings)

It is important to determine the intent when establishing the measurement system. At this point of process effort, the concern is to get a snapshot of current process performance. Ideally, that snapshot should be on the same metrics that will most likely be implemented in the improved process. The difference between the snapshot and future view is simply the approach taken in gathering the information. In the snapshot view, the approach needs to be quick and painless. Most likely, this will require gathering information manually, limiting time through a sample of only a few occurrences, and blending together existing information to create the measurement data needed. In the future state, when the new process is running, the approach needs to be ongoing, automated, and institutionalized. The measures of the future state also need to be linked with process goals as well as reliable and presented in a fashion that enables systematic evaluation and improvement.

BENCHMARK THE PROCESS

At this point of the effort there is an understanding of the current process. Measures of efficiency and effectiveness that are most valuable to the effort have been identified. Soon the team will begin to make significant improvements to accomplish the process objectives. Before proceeding, it is wise to ask a few basic questions. Just how much should the process change? Are the future targets and objectives adequate for the business? Are there ideas to be gained from other people or companies? Answers to these questions can be obtained through benchmarking.

As defined by International Benchmarking Clearinghouse, "Benchmarking is a systematic and continuous measurement process; a process of continuously comparing and measuring an organization's business [or IS] processes against business leaders anywhere in the world to gain information which helps the organization take action to improve its performance." In business, a benchmark is the imprint of the highest performer of a process, a performance example for others to follow. Through benchmarking, a company identifies gaps in its own performance and targets areas for improvement. Benchmarking is a tool for continuous improvement and must be an ongoing process, as industry benchmarks can change radically in six months time due to advancements in technology.

There are many reasons to benchmark metrics and processes against the industry.

- It is a tool for continuous improvement and can provide stimulation for change as the organization strives for excellence.
- It can provide a sense of urgency for change. It can motivate companies into taking action and improving their situation. When one company sees another company perform a process faster, better, or with less cost, the first company can see it has an opportunity for improvement.
- It can stimulate innovation, creativity, and outside-the-box thinking to discover new ways of improving processes.
- It can motivate quantum improvement and re-engineering rather than incremental, continuous improvement.
- It forces a thorough understanding of one's own processes.

There are also several areas of caution when undertaking a benchmarking exercise.

- Make sure the benchmarking is specific and know why.
- Ensure that the process owner is on-board. If the sponsor of the benchmarking is someone other than the process owner, ensure there is full buy-in and understanding.
- Involve those who will be implementing the change. Also involve individuals outside of the process, particularly those who receive output or provide input to the process.

- Ensure that process flows and maps are understood and documented thoroughly and completely. Full agreement on the representation of the current process should be obtained before looking at benchmarks.
- Ensure the selection of appropriate benchmarking companies to obtain valid comparisons, benchmark against the best, not the most convenient.
- Be sure to compare like processes. The metrics and components should be measured alike.
- Devote sufficient time for the benchmarking process. Benchmarking can be a time-consuming activity. Take sufficient time for planning, documenting, training, and involving others.
- Keep the focus and scope of the benchmarking study small and simple. Ensure that everyone understands the objective of the benchmarking exercise.
- Prepare properly for the site visits or benchmarking questionnaires. A weak questionnaire can result in insufficient or inconclusive information. Structured visits result in the most information and value.
- Thoroughly collect quantitative data to allow for valid comparisons with benchmarking partners.
- Collect qualitative data on how various processes are done and why they are done that way.
- Be prepared to share information openly with the benchmarking partners and have something to offer the partner in return.
- Improve the process, not just the metric for sustaining results. Metrics by themselves do not correct problems.

As outlined in Figure 7.6, there are three different ways of approaching benchmarking.

- **Internal Benchmarking.** Often, an organization offers its own good benchmarking environment. There are processes in other departments that may have similar output, purpose, or intents. These processes may not provide a target number or value to obtain, but they will provide a perspective on different approaches available. This type of benchmarking is generally the easiest to perform.
- **Operational Benchmarking.** This type of benchmarking is usually most effective. Many companies are doing innovative and new things and it may not be necessary to find a world-class benchmark to generate effective ideas and targets for the organization. Contact associates, suppliers, or even companies highlighted in recent publications. Value can often be found in areas much closer than first realized.

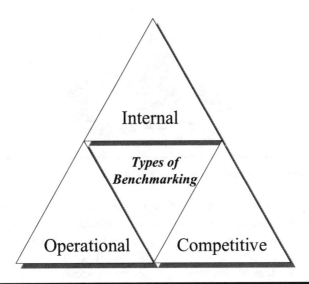

Figure 7.6 Types of Benchmarking

■ **Competitive Benchmarking.** Of the three different benchmarking techniques, competitive benchmarking is the most difficult. Unlike competitive products, which can be bought and torn apart to learn from, competitive processes are difficult to assess without being onsite. Couple this with sensitivity, security, and confidentiality issues and it becomes an experience that may waste more time than the value provided. It may be necessary to get creative. Some performance metrics can be estimated from financial statements and other publicly filed documents.

No matter which approach is chosen, benchmarking should include the following activities:

■ Determining what to benchmark
■ Determining quantifiable measures and techniques to compare
■ Contacting the benchmark partner and describe the intent and desired outcomes
■ Visiting and performing the benchmark, understanding and analyzing the best practice and benchmarking partners process
■ Analyzing gaps between the present process and the benchmark process
■ Adapting and implementing better or improved practices into the process redesign.

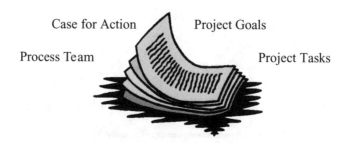

Case for Action   Project Goals

Process Team   Project Tasks

Figure 7.7 Elements of Successful Process Plans

Benchmarking is an important step of the process improvement effort. Do not underestimate the value of what might be learned. The benchmarking effort will provide new targets, techniques, metrics, and designs for the future process. It will also confirm that the efforts are on track and seed new ideas for improving different processes.

DEVELOP PROCESS PLAN

Good planning will help the process improvement effort succeed. This requires an understanding of project planning techniques. In Chapter 3, many of these project planning techniques are described in the context of the overall process improvement initiative. Now, the desire is to apply these planning steps to a specific process improvement effort. As shown in Figure 7.7, the following elements are critical to a successful process improvement project plan, and it is now time to review how the process team, Case for Action, and process tasks come together to form the process plan.

- **Process Team:** Every process initiative needs a team of people to accomplish the goals. Earlier we were introduced to the project team that organized the entire process initiative. Now it is time to organize a process team that will focus on a specific process. This process team is at the center of the process change. The team will evaluate the current process, explore ideas, then create and implement a new process. This team will facilitate the implementation of the process change; therefore, members need to be carefully selected. Invite the strongest supporters and the biggest critics of the particular process. There are good ideas that come from an exchange among people who have different perspectives. Figure 7.8 highlights this team. Consider the following roles and responsibilities when forming the process team:

  1. **Process Sponsor:** The sponsor establishes the vision of the process for the future. He or she communicates the purpose of

Figure 7.8 Process Team

addressing the process and what benefits can be achieved. The sponsor has the passion and motivation for the process to make the re-engineering effort survive through tough times. The sponsor must have authority and responsibility to get resources, foster involvement, and make decisions on a particular process. Typically, this person would be someone from the process steering team. The sponsor will also keep the vision intact from a customer perspective.

2. **Facilitator:** The facilitator ensures a productive and safe environment for the project team. The facilitator is the catalyst who helps the team members think outside the box while also keeping the discussion on task. This person should be a neutral party not directly impacted by the process being designed.

3. **Suppliers:** These would include individuals who provide input into the information systems process.

4. **Customers:** Customers are individuals who receive the output from the information systems process.

5. **Process Participants:** Participants include those directly involved in the process to be improved or re-engineered.

6. **Technicians:** These are individuals with expertise regarding technology.

7. **Scribe:** The scribe is responsible for taking and distributing notes from all the meetings and discussions. This includes following up on action items to ensure closure. The scribe is responsible for developing process flow diagrams based on discussions.

■ **Case for Action:** It is through the Case for Action that the need and vision for dramatic process change is articulated. As previously discussed, there are six components that should be included in the Case

- Environment
- Problem
- Demands
- Diagnosis
- Cost of Inaction
- Objectives

Figure 7.9 Case for Action Components

for Action. These are demonstrated in Figure 7.9. With a simple change of perspective these same components are valid at the process level.

1. **Environment:** This describes what is happening or what has changed to cause concern with the current process.
2. **Problem:** In consideration of the process, the problem states the source of the organization's concerns.
3. **Demands:** The suppliers and customers of the process expect certain outcomes, and the goals of the process need to be aligned with these expectations.
4. **Diagnosis:** This explains why the current process is unable to meet the demands of the suppliers and customers.
5. **Cost of Inaction:** This identifies the consequence of staying *as is*.
6. **Objectives:** The objectives of the process improvement effort should be clearly defined and demonstrate how these efforts will meet the expectations.

An example of a specific process improvement Case for Action is shown in Figure 7.10.

■ **Process Tasks:** A process plan also includes tasks or work assignments that detail what needs to get done. Tasks are specific steps to follow to accomplish the goals. For example, "interview process

---

Case for Action
Understanding Business Needs Process

Our organization has experienced growing competitive pressures and lackluster business revenue over the last six months. These changes have forced most managers to seek additional information to help make critical business decisions for their function.

This change has created a rush of increased programming requests for the Information Systems Department. Today programming requests are managed informally. Priorities are often adjusted based on the requester's ability to "sell" the need. There is a tendency in Information Systems to address innovative and interesting projects. Such behavior often shifts work from one project to another. In the end it appears that nothing ever gets done. With the existing revenue pressures, the opportunity to expand programming capacities does not exist. Therefore, a solution needs to be implemented to understand business needs.

This lack of a formalized business need process is frustrating for department managers. Each person expects his requests to be addressed, yet they understand the need to work on projects based on need and value to the organization. At the core, these "customers" demand consistency in how those priority decisions are made. They also want to be informed and kept abreast of those decisions and any changes.

The existing process is unable to meet these new demands. There is no process defined. There are no set techniques to understand and evaluate needs and priorities.

Should the Information Systems group continue to work in this ad hoc manner, the consequences will be increased frustration among managers and programming staff as well as missed value and opportunities.

The objective of this process improvement effort is to establish a formalized business need process that includes: a priority system based on measurable criteria, a communicated response back to a requester within three working days of a request, and an ongoing list of projects and activities in priority order.

Figure 7.10 Process Improvement Case for Action

participants" is a task. Tasks are assigned to specific groups or individuals. Each task will have a schedule or timeline attached to it. Start and end dates define the timeline for each task and provide the measure of progress toward completing the project. It is important to recognize the difference between duration and work time. *Duration* is the amount of time between the start and end dates. It does not mean the amount of time that work gets done on the project. Duration is elapsed time. For example, if interviews are conducted for a process improvement project between the 12th and 24th of the month, there is a duration of 12 days. The amount of time actually doing interviews, for example 13 hours, is called *work time*. Scheduling duration on project plans and tracking work time should be done separately for reporting, summarizing, and planning resources.

■ Besides an end date, the completion of a task may further be defined by the outcomes of the task. These outcomes are called *deliverables*. Deliverables are a way for a project manager to define what he/she wants out of a certain task. The *deliverable* may be a Summary Report, a Flowchart, a Listing, etc. Anything that is produced as a result of a task is called a *deliverable*. During the project planning phase, define these deliverables should be defined along with the tasks.

PITFALLS TO AVOID

■ **Defining vague objectives:** The objectives of the process effort need to be specific. This helps team members, process participants, management, and customers clearly understand the intent of the process. If the objectives are vague there will be confusion, unfulfilled expectations, and potential conflict. Objectives should be specific.

■ **Not measuring the right metric:** When establishing baseline measures, the right set of metrics must be selected. Metrics support either effectiveness or efficiency. Do not try to measure the effectiveness of the process by putting in metrics that actually support efficiency. It is important to consider how the knowledge gained from each measure will actually be used.

■ **Skipping baseline data:** It is easy to shift attention from the current process to the new one and get distracted from gathering essential baseline data. No doubt, somebody will have issues with the new and improved process. By gathering critical pieces of baseline data we can support the changes which need to be made.

■ **Benchmarks not measuring similar processes:** Benchmark data can be deceiving if not obtained and used in a proper fashion. There should be an understanding of what is being benchmarked and compared. Critical factors and conditions need to be similar between both processes to draw valuable conclusions.

KEY POINTS TO REMEMBER

■ Process objectives establish the vision for what the process needs to become.

■ Process metrics are used to help guide the improvement initiative. There are two types: efficiency and effectiveness.

■ Baseline data is collected to obtain an understanding of the current process performance and define the objectives of the new process effort.

- Benchmarking is used for comparing process performance and establishing improvement objectives.
- Deliverables for Step 5, Process Plan, include:
  - Process objectives
  - Process metrics and baseline data
  - Industry and benchmark notes
  - Process plan with Case for Action

NOTES AND IDEAS FOR MY PROCESS IMPROVEMENT EFFORT

8

FUTURE STATE PROCESS MAPPING

"If you can dream it, you can do it."

Walt Disney

The new and improved process is finally ready to be developed. The Case for Action has been completed and the team is ready to move ahead with ideas and suggestions. The next step is designing the future state. Following are the tasks in this step:

- **Identify Process Owner**
  - Responsibilities of a process owner
  - Characteristics of a process owner
- **Organize Redesign Sessions**
  - Gathering the right people
  - Gathering the information
- **Develop New Process**
  - Improve or reengineer the process
  - Brainstorming
  - Redesign techniques
  - Best practices
  - Future state flowchart
- **Validate New Process**
  - Competing elements
  - Business factors
  - Efficiency and effectiveness
  - Issue Resolution

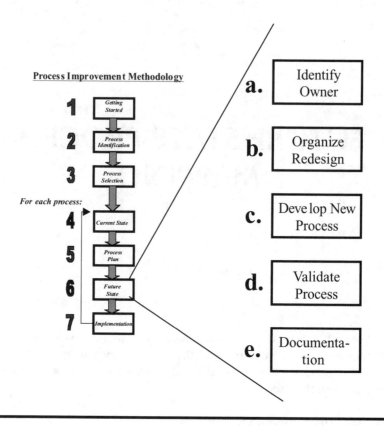

Figure 8.1 Future State

- Risk analysis
- **Develop Process Documentation**

The tasks are shown in Figure 8.1.

IDENTIFY PROCESS OWNER

Waiting until now to identify a process owner allows us to observe the initial process improvement effort and determine who may be best for the critical role of process owner. However, it is important to select the individual before the redesign of the new process so he or she can own the new process beginning with the redesign efforts.

Responsibilities of a Process Owner

The process owner is an individual who is responsible for the overall process, including the redesign as well as the ongoing operation of the process. In addition to guiding the improvement efforts, it is the process owner who has ultimate responsibility for the efficient and effective operation of the process. Without a process owner, the neglectful old ways of process management will quickly return and erode the integrity of the new process.

It is critical that the process owner owns the process totally, even across organizational silos. Although process participants may be exposed to only one portion of the process, the process owner is the person who can ensure that all the pieces of the process function together. This is critical, as each person or group may claim that their particular piece of the process is functioning properly, yet in reality the process as a whole may not be meeting the objectives or operating effectively.

In most organizations, the process owner does not have direct management responsibility over the people who perform work in the process. The traditional manager retains management responsibility over these individuals. However, the process owner must have real responsibility for and authority over the functioning of the process. Rather than focusing on the management of the people, the process owner can focus on designing the process, executing it, measuring the process performance, and managing the interactions with other processes. It may be a challenge to get the functional managers to change their style of management and accept the involvement of a process owner, as this involvement could uncover practices that some managers may prefer to leave alone. However, traditional management techniques of command and control will not work well in a process culture. Management success relies on the techniques of cooperation, negotiation, and openness. It is imperative to foster this environment through training, coaching, mentoring, and communicating; help the traditional manager adjust to a process owner; and work to ensure the success of this valuable partnership.

The specific roles and responsibilities of the process owner are shown in Figure 8.2. The initial responsibilities are

- Guiding the process improvement effort toward the defined goals
- Limiting the range of the improvement effort to the scope of the project
- Organizing team members to contribute facts and data and to participate in the redesign
- Overcoming barriers to improvement
- Considering the impacts on other processes and collaborating with other process owners to harmonize and avoid conflicts
- Championing the implementation
- Surveying customers of the process to ensure satisfaction
- Adjusting the process based on business and technology changes

Initial		Ongoing
• **Guide the redesign effort**		• **Manage process end to end**
• **Keep within scope**		• **Process knowledge & vision**
• **Organize data**		• **Improve efficiency**
• **Overcome barriers**		• **Improve effectiveness**
• **Consider impacts**		• **Monitor**
• **Champion implementation**		• **Lead, influence, motivate**
• **Survey customers**		• **Manage interfaces**
• **Adjust the process**		• **Communicate**
		• **Request resources**
		• **Monitor process metrics**
		• **Communicate results**
		• **Initiate improvement**

Figure 8.2 Process Owner Responsibilities

On an ongoing basis, the process owner has the following roles and responsibilities:

- Owning and managing the process from end to end
- Having knowledge of the process and a vision of how it should function
- Being committed to the efficiency and effectiveness of the process
- Being involved with and monitoring the functioning of the process
- Leading, influencing, and motivating process participants, but not necessarily managing process participants
- Managing process interfaces with other processes
- Communicating, collaborating, and negotiating with other process owners
- Requesting additional resources when necessary
- Monitoring process metrics
- Communicating process results to the organization
- Initiating improvement efforts when necessary

Characteristics of a Process Owner

As shown in Figure 8.3, there are some specific personal skills that a process owner must possess. These include:

- Personal motivation and tolerance for change within the organization
- Knowledge of process improvement principles, methodologies, and tools
- Administration skills, including planning, organizing, and prioritizing

Personal motivation

Interpersonal skills

Process improvement knowledge

Administration skills

Analysis, problem solving

Leadership skills

Figure 8.3 Process Owner Personal Skills

- Leadership skills, including the ability to motivate and influence others, establish a vision, delegate, coach and train, and command respect
- Interpersonal and communication skills, including listening, conflict resolution, oral and written formal and informal communication, and building relationships
- Analysis and problem-solving skills and ability to identify problems and alternatives, make sound and timely decisions, and analyze risk

Although the process owners will not have these skills immediately, this list should be used to develop and grow their areas of expertise.

ORGANIZE REDESIGN SESSIONS

Now that the process owner has been identified, it is time to organize the redesign sessions, including gathering the right people to be involved and gathering all the information that will be needed in preparation for the redesign sessions.

Gathering the Right People

It is important to work with the process owner to select the individuals to be involved in the process redesign sessions. Several different groups need to be represented in the redesign session:

- **Team Members:** Team members who gathered the current state information attend and provide an understanding of the current process and related issues.
- **Process Participants:** Process participants involved in the redesign effort express ideas and solutions based on their detailed understanding of the process and gain ownership in the new process.

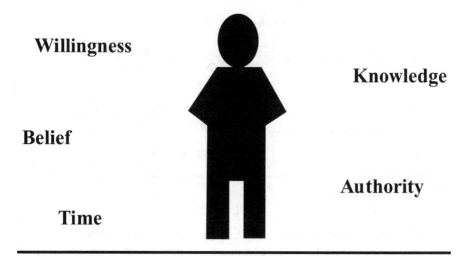

Figure 8.4 Process Redesign Participant Characteristics

- **Process Customers:** It can be helpful to have the customer of the process attend the redesign session to provide clarity on the requirements.
- **Interfacing Process Owners:** If the process has key interfacing points with other processes, it can be useful to involve the other process owners in the redesign session.

Although it may be tempting to involve a large number of people in the redesign session, due to logistics and group dynamics, the number of people who actually attend the redesign session should be limited. The ideal size of the redesign group is from five to eight individuals. Having fewer than five individuals limits the range of ideas, while having more than eight individuals leaves some individuals on the sidelines unable to fully participate. You can always involve additional individuals in the review of the new process resulting from the redesign sessions.

Each participant in the redesign session needs to possess the following characteristics as shown by Figure 8.4:

- A willingness to participate
- A belief in the Case for Action
- Time to commit to meeting to design the new solution
- Knowledge of the process
- Authority to make decisions

By combining the right people with the right knowledge, the foundation for an effective redesign session is established.

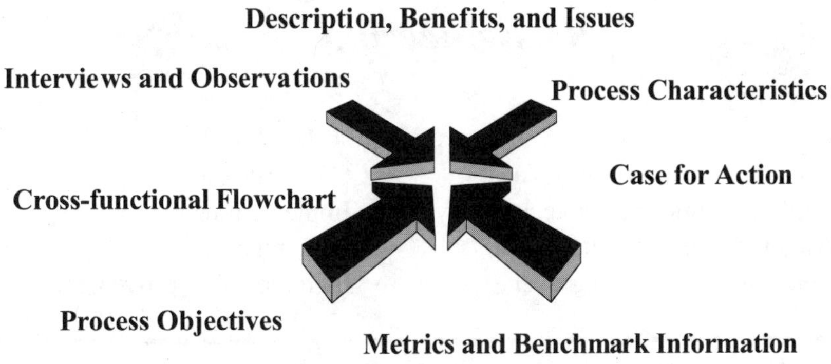

Description, Benefits, and Issues

Interviews and Observations

Process Characteristics

Cross-functional Flowchart

Case for Action

Process Objectives

Metrics and Benchmark Information

Figure 8.5 Process Information to Gather

Gathering the Information

At this point in the improvement effort, a substantial amount of information concerning the process has been developed and is gathered and reviewed by all team members in preparation for the redesign session. This information is identified in Figure 8.5 and includes:

- **Process Description, Benefits, and Issues:** When all the processes were identified, a brief description, benefits, and issues were developed for the process. This information should be reviewed with the team so they understand an overview of the process.
- **Interview and Observation Information:** When beginning work on this particular process, individuals were interviewed and the process was observed to obtain additional information. This information needs to be reviewed with all team members so they have a thorough understanding of the current process.
- **Cross-Functional Flowchart:** To ensure that participants understand the detailed current process flow, the current state process flowchart that was developed should be reviewed.
- **Process Objectives:** To ensure everyone understands the vision and goals, objectives of the new process should be reviewed.
- **Metrics and Benchmark Information:** Metrics and baseline data were compared with benchmark information and should be reviewed with the team.
- **Case for Action:** This document is used to communicate to the team the passion, need, and purpose of improving the process.
- **Process Characteristics:** Characteristics of a good process were discussed in the beginning of this book and identified in

Reengineering

Is...	*Is NOT...*
• A fundamental process redesign	• Corporate downsizing
• Exploiting information technology	• Implementing computer systems
• Aligning structure with processes	• Flattening the company structure
• Reinventing or starting over	• Incremental improvement

Figure 8.6 Reengineering

Appendix A. This list should be consulted to guide the development of the new process.

DEVELOP NEW PROCESS

After identifying a process owner and the right individuals to involve for gathering and reviewing the process information, it is now time to develop the new process. The temptation to jump straight into developing a new process has been resisted by following the steps outlined in this book. Now the benefits of this work can be reaped and a new process developed that is efficient, effective, and meets the objectives.

Improve or Reengineer the Process

The team must begin developing the process by making a decision to either improve or reengineer the process. Understanding the difference between improving and reengineering the process is important.

Improving a process involves implementing incremental change to make the process better. Improving recognizes that the basic structure of a process is solid and that the performance can be enhanced and optimized through incremental change. The aim is to do what is already being done, only better. The key is steady incremental improvement.

Reengineering is the fundamental rethinking and redesign of a process to achieve dramatic improvements. Reengineering ignores today's process and concentrates on what should be done for tomorrow. All structures and procedures are reinvented, not improved, not enhanced, not modified. It is starting over with a blank piece of paper and asking, "What do I need to do to meet the needs of my customers/users?" When

Think about the future   Have fun!

Focus on the process   Encourage involvement

                                        Have an open mind
Concentrate on the
     solution   Generate ideas

Respond to the question   Don't criticize

     Consider every solution   Talk about things to do

Figure 8.7 Redesign Session Team Guidelines

re-engineering, one must not be hampered with the constraints of today. Figure 8.6 highlights what reengineering is, and what it is not.

Brainstorming

To obtain ideas during the redesign sessions, the team will utilize brainstorming. As with any brainstorming session, keeping all of the members participating, on track, polite, and effective can be a challenge. Following are guidelines for the brainstorming session as shown in Figure 8.7:

- Think and talk about the future, not the past
- Focus on the process, not the people
- Concentrate on the solution, not the problem
- Respond to the question, not the person
- Consider every solution, not every mistake
- Talk about the things to do, not what did not get done
- Be accepting of ideas, not critical
- Focus on generating ideas, not organizing them
- Have an open mind
- Encourage involvement from everyone
- Have fun

Some questions to ask about the process in the redesign sessions include:

- Do we know enough about the purpose of the process and the process details to effectively redesign the process?
- Are the right people involved to design the process?

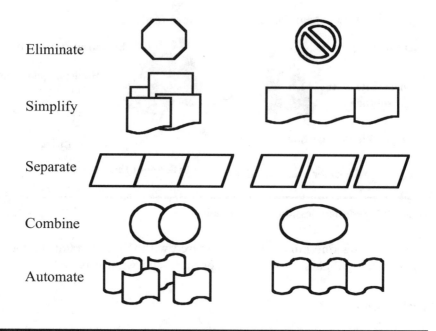

Eliminate

Simplify

Separate

Combine

Automate

Figure 8.8 Process Improvement Redesign Techniques

- How do we achieve the benefits identified for the process?
- Can the issues with the process be avoided?
- Can the issues in the process identified earlier be tolerated?
- If the issues cannot be tolerated, what must change in the process to eliminate the issues?
- Can the probability that the issues will occur be reduced?
- Can the impact of the issues be reduced?

The members of the redesign team will define the future process, consolidating the information they need, blending their experience, fostering creativity, and encouraging idea generation. They will target their process knowledge toward a solution that effectively and efficiently meets the objective of the process. Several redesign sessions may be needed to reach the desired result.

Redesign Techniques

There are five process improvement redesign techniques that can guide the brainstorming effort to improve the performance of the process. As Figure 8.8 describes, these five techniques are: Eliminate, Simplify, Separate, Combine, and Automate. A discussion of each process improvement redesign technique follows.

Eliminate process steps.

Processes are composed of steps. In the existing process, some of the steps may add value, and some may not. As the team begins to brainstorm process improvements, one of the largest opportunities is to eliminate work that does not add value. Non-value added steps do not directly move a process forward and do not directly add to the output required by the customer. Activities of this type include, but are not limited to, moving, searching, waiting, reworking, and sorting. The initial focus should be to eliminate these types of non-value added activities. Ask the following questions:

- Does the step really need to be done?
- Can the step do less?
- Can something be omitted?
- Can some activity be deleted without harming the process output?
- Does this step add any value?
- Would the customer pay to have this step completed?

Good process work begins by attacking the waste first, rather than the work. Elimination of these steps will be an effective start to a new and improved process.

Simplify process steps.

Processes can quickly become complex within Information Systems. At first, a few simple steps are linked together, but soon this linkage expands to involve other steps and people. The people on the team all have different needs, from knowing exactly what is going on at any time to tracking abnormalities in the process. To guide and monitor the process often requires implementing new technologies. New technologies require new skills. These new skills require training. Training requires more clarity in the requirements. And on and on. A process can quickly become complex. It becomes difficult to understand the flow, make decisions, learn, and even change. It becomes difficult to actually do all of the steps of a process. When a process is simplified, these issues are reduced. To simplify the process, ask these questions:

- Is there another option or another flow?
- Can steps be reordered?
- Can steps be simplified?
- What changes can be made to shorten the time?
- Is there a different way?
- Can we do less?

Simple processes have fewer steps, fewer people, and fewer issues. Less is more. So, it is important to brainstorm ways to simplify every step of the process and do less.

Separate process steps.

After brainstorming ways to eliminate and simplify steps of a process, opportunities to separate steps of the process need to be identified. Separation helps reduce complexity. Questions to ask include:

- What steps could be regrouped?
- Who could do the steps instead?
- Where are there natural breaks in the process?
- What steps could be shifted?
- What steps can be separated?

Often, separation involves creating alternative parallel paths. These parallel paths improve a process by reducing the process cycle time. Brainstorming ways to separate steps is a way to improve the overall performance of the process.

Combine process steps.

Not every step can be eliminated, simplified, or even separated. More often than not, actually combining process steps is an effective improvement technique. By combining steps we can reduce the number of people involved in the process, eliminate the waste between the steps (like delays or waits), and build quality into the process. When brainstorming, questions to ask include:

- What steps can be combined?
- How much can be combined?
- Who could do the combined work?
- Can steps be reshuffled or rearranged together?
- What other steps could come together?

The focus on combining steps is to make the process more productive. Brainstorm every combination and we will be one step closer to an effective process redesign.

Automate process steps.

The last brainstorming technique focuses on the automation of process steps. This technique is listed last because it is the last area to brainstorm.

We live in an information age. The fact that you are reading this book means you know that information systems can provide effective business solutions. But be careful. Resist the tendency to jump into process improvements by implementing automated technology first. Automating an existing poor process with computers, networks, and databases will still yield poor results, only more quickly. Therefore, we need to look for the best opportunities to apply automation. Computers are critical in managing many aspects of the process, from supplier to customer. Computers are helpful in digesting information about processes and helping decide on a future direction. But we should keep in mind the process objectives and look for ways to enable technology within information systems processes.

These techniques can be used to create a redesigned process. However, do not over analyze or try to redesign the perfect process. It is better to make a good decision at the right time than a perfect decision too late.

Best Practices

The redesign techniques discussed above will assist in developing the very best process possible for the organization. But how much change is really necessary or possible? What is the world-class standard for the process?

Best processes require an understanding of best practices. Best practices are specific activities that produce a desired outcome better than anything else can. Best practices optimize costs, quality, and time to reach a result that exceeds customer expectations. Once explored, best practices provide ideas for how the process should be redesigned.

Processes that are best practices excel in all areas. Customer measures are specific, show positive trends, and generate improvement actions. Internal process measures have positive trends, stretch targets, and no errors. Process training exists and is continually refined to meet the needs of the employee. Documentation is current and completed using world-class standards. Benchmarking is ongoing and used to set targets and gauge performance of both process and customer measures. And finally, the process is continually improved through use of data and documented actions.

With all of these considerations, identifying a best practice is a challenge. It is also difficult to prove that the process is the best that can be found. Realize that the pursuit of best practices can be time consuming and expensive. Benchmarking trips to Cisco, Dell, Amazon.com, and Microsoft sound good but are difficult to execute. One option is to engage outside companies to provide research and assistance. But, of course, there is still nothing like being onsite to observe processes firsthand.

Figure 8.9 Process Impacts to Consider

When returning from a benchmarking trip with valuable ideas, keep in mind that piecemeal copying may not create the necessary benefit. What is a best practice in one organization may be a failure in another. It is important to consider the requirements of each individual company. As shown by Figure 8.9, some of the items that impact a process include:

- Culture of the company
- Culture of the Information Systems organization
- Skill level of process participants
- Profile of users
- Standards and procedures
- Complexity of technology used
- Position of the organization on the process evolution model
- Leadership
- Business objectives
- Information Systems objectives
- Budget
- Staff size and availability
- Complexity of the process
- Industry trends and technology available at the time

Another way to obtain additional ideas is by referencing a list of best practices. Following are some of the best practices that are common across all information systems processes.

- **Standardize:** Process steps, tools, and components in the architecture are standardized as much as possible. Processes use common standards and enforcement of the standards.
- **Integrate:** Processes, steps, tools, and information are integrated whenever possible. Redundant databases and steps are eliminated. Cross-process branching and interfacing with other processes is reduced as much as possible.
- **Simplify:** Process steps are simplified, eliminating unnecessary tasks and performing only value-added activities.
- **Commoditize:** Processes are well defined, well understood, and well known. Process skills are identified, and the process drives homogeneity. Process steps are normalized and repeatable.
- **Event driven:** Event-driven processes are triggered automatically based on rules or predetermined parameters.
- **Exception driven:** Processes are designed for the 80/20 rule, or to handle the majority of the flow seamlessly and quickly. The 20 percent emergency or exceptions will follow a different process flow or route.
- **Modular:** Processes are split into smaller parts so the process is more adaptable. It is easier to change details without changing the whole process flow. Subprocesses can be reused in other process branches.
- **Reuse:** Several processes have common functions that can be reused for productivity, consistency, and quality.
- **Automate:** Tools are added to the process to automate flow and functionality. Tools are integrated across tightly coupled processes. Automation will reduce costs in the process.
- **Consistent:** The process is followed consistently by all members. Management support exists to ensure consistent application rather than individual treatment.
- **Closed loop:** There is no work-around to the process. The process covers all of the steps from beginning to end.
- **Real time:** Processes are designed for real-time information rather than reporting after the fact. With current information, corrective action can be taken.
- **Documented:** The process is documented and the documentation is up to date with how the process functions.
- **Measured:** Metrics are used to measure the process and encourage continuous improvement. Reports are reviewed on a regular basis. Ideal metrics are business-coupled metrics.
- **Proactive:** Processes are designed to project, forecast, and model so that action can be taken before an event occurs.

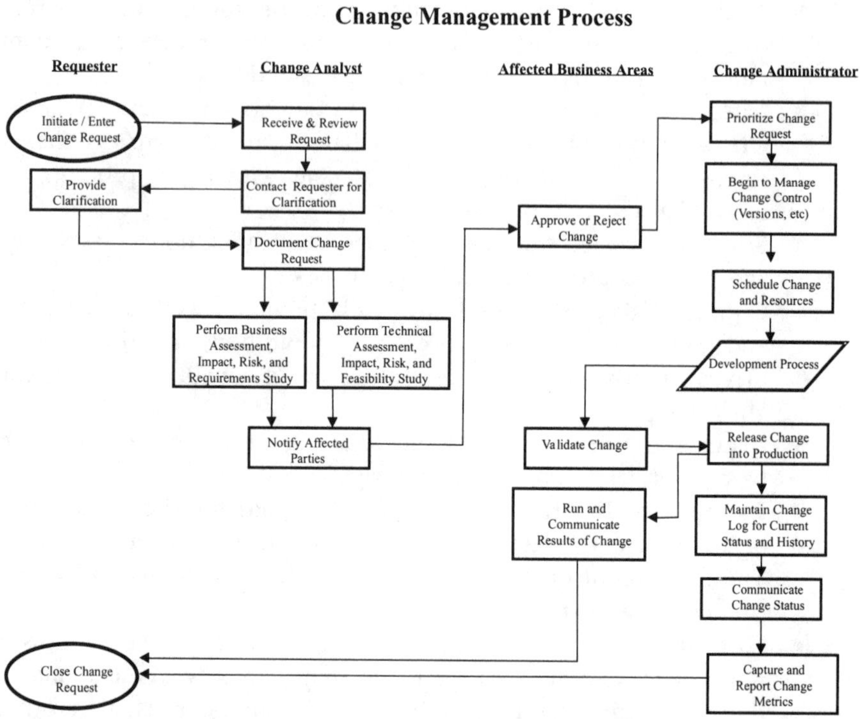

Change Management Process

Figure 8.10 Change Management Process Flowchart

- **Customer intimacy:** Processes are designed to provide a total solution for the customer.
- **E-enabled:** Processes are designed to consider the impact of e-business. Ensure every channel the customers use is easy and consistent. Use the Internet and web tools whenever possible.

The above best practices span all processes. Appendix H outlines a checklist of design components that should be considered for each individual process. Although process designs and process components change as technology and needs change, these design components are typically found in the processes of world-class organizations.

Future State Flowchart

The documented outcome of the new and improved process is a cross-functional flowchart. The details of this flowcharting technique are covered in Chapter 6. For the future state flowchart apply the same standards. The new flowchart represents a consolidation of brainstorm-

Service Level Management Process

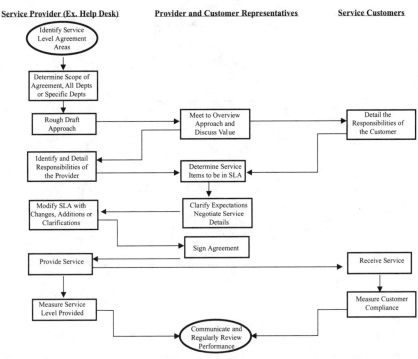

Figure 8.11 Service Level Management Process Flowchart

ing ideas, best practice guidelines, assessment elements, and good teamwork. The flowchart is used to generate consensus and develop the new process. It is also used to communicate the new process to team members, participants, and management. Figures 8.10 and 8.11 highlight examples of portions of two information system processes at a company.

VALIDATE NEW PROCESS

Once the team has established a new design that has incorporated best practices, the new design must be validated. Validation brings us back to the basic requirements of the process. It is a check of the redesigned process to ensure that the goals and business factors of the process have been addressed in the redesign. The following ways to validate a process are discussed:

■ Competing elements
■ Business factors

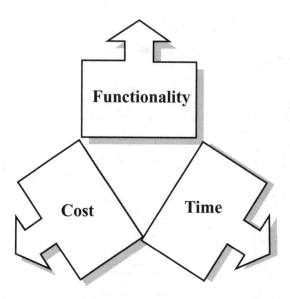

Figure 8.12 Competing Process Elements

■ Efficiency and effectiveness
■ Issue resolution
■ Risk analysis

Competing Elements

Redesigning the new process is often a compromise among three elements: time, cost, and functionality. Unfortunately, the process effort can optimize two of these elements, but typically not all three. Figure 8.12 demonstrates this optimization trade off. Optimizing the time and costs of the process initiative will probably limit functionality, which may include reliability. Extending the process effort to increase functionality and more costs will surely be incurred. Each element needs to be considered as the process is defined. The elements must be balanced to an appropriate level. Although the best practices outlined above provide groundwork, if the compromise is too great, good is sometimes better than best. Again, it is better to make a good decision at the right time than a perfect decision too late.

Business Factors

Earlier in Chapter 5, a set of business factors was defined that were used to select the process for improvement or redesign. These same factors are

Inventory and Asset Management Process			
Business Factor	*Accomplishes Objective*		
	N/A	NO	YES
Generates Revenue	✓		
Contains Costs			✓
Improves Productivity			✓
Supports Strategy	✓		
Ensures Operations	✓		
Improves Flexibility			✓

Figure 8.13 Process Validation

now used to validate that the redesign has accomplished its intent, including the ability of the process to:

- Generate revenue
- Contain costs
- Improve productivity
- Support strategy
- Ensure operations
- Improve flexibility

Figure 8.13 demonstrates how the checklist used to select the process can also be modified to validate the process as well.

Now is also the time to look at the original process objectives and Case for Action. Will the objectives of the redesign be achieved?

Efficiency and Effectiveness

In addition to the business factors, the redesign must withstand scrutiny against the measurements of efficiency and effectiveness. Each of these elements should be revisited to assure that the redesigned process is indeed the best it can be and that the redesign has incorporated the characteristics of a good process that are included in Appendix A.

Issue Resolution

During process validation, it is important to confirm that the process redesign is fixing the fundamental process issues, and not just the symptoms. For example, a continuously high backlog of programming requests may seem to signal the need for additional resources (a symptom) when the real issue is how requests are evaluated and accepted (the root cause). Although symptomatic solutions are quicker to apply, they are only temporary. Such well-intended solutions may make matters worse over the long term. Opting for symptomatic solutions is enticing, because apparent improvement is achieved and pressure to improve is relieved. However, easing a problem symptom also reduces any perceived need to find a more fundamental solution. Meanwhile, the underlying problem remains and may worsen, and the side effects of the symptomatic solution make it still harder to apply the fundamental solution. It is critical to question each process solution and tie it back to root cause, not symptoms.

Risk Analysis

Before finalizing the process redesign, the risks with the new process need to identified and analyzed. Any new process will have some risks associated with the change. Risk taking is essential to progress and an important part of learning; however, it is important to identify and recognize the risks in advance. Once the risks are understood, we may choose to modify the new process or to accept the risks and manage them during the implementation of the new process. It is important to communicate the risks of the new process up the chain of command to management, as well as down to the individuals involved in the process.

There may be several different categories of risks associated with the new process, such as those associated with:

- The time element of the tasks in the new process
- The resources required for implementation
- The resources required for the new process itself
- The scope of the new process
- Tasks that cannot be easily measured

Some things to look for when analyzing the risks associated with time, include:

- Tasks in the process that take longer than one week, or more than 15 percent of the total process cycle time

- Tasks on the critical path of the process
- Tasks that have several predecessors in the process
- Tasks that are overly complex
- Tasks that are extremely variable in time
- Tasks with tight time frames
- Tasks with unrealistic time estimates

When analyzing risks relative to resources, we need to look for the following:

- Tasks that require a large amount of resources
- Tasks that require a specific skill set or a scarce skill set
- Tasks heavily dependent on one person
- Tasks that rely on external resources or groups
- Limited availability of tools or automation to support the tasks
- Risks associated with technology

Some risks relative to scope include:

- Tasks of the process that interface with the business
- Tasks that are critical to meeting performance metrics identified
- Tasks that rely on business input, areas outside of Information Systems' direct control

There are three different ways to minimize the risk:

- **Reduce the risk:** Reduce the probability that the situation will happen or minimize the impact the risk will have.
- **Transfer the risk:** Move or shift the risk to another area or party.
- **Avoid the risk:** Take a different action completely, with less risk.

To mitigate the areas of risk:

- Design redundancy into the process
- Add resources
- Cross-train resources
- Schedule high-risk tasks early in the process
- Have proper controls or reviews in place for the high-risk areas
- Eliminate high-risk tasks
- Prototype or test the new process
- Add or remove technology

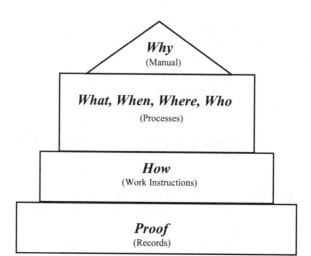

Figure 8.14 Documentation Structure

DEVELOP PROCESS DOCUMENTATION

Documentation is the written or graphic representation of a process. As we have all experienced in other areas, there is a difference between ineffective documentation and useful documentation. There is also a balance between too little documentation and too much. To make documentation of any process successful we must first understand why the documentation is needed. There are several important reasons to document a process. Documentation:

- Acts as a guide to how the process works best
- Defines the requirements of the process
- Clarifies responsibilities
- Ensures accountability to the process
- Demonstrates that the process is understood
- Communicates to others what the process does
- Helps train and instruct others on how the process works
- Includes information required by each area

With an understanding of why process documentation is important, you are able to understand the need for a documentation structure. Figure 8.14 demonstrates a documentation structure suitable for information systems processes.

At the highest level, the documentation structure consists of a definition of why processes and activities are being done. This is a higher level view of the information systems organization and is broad enough to encompass all aspects of the operation. The documentation is written and includes text, diagrams, and graphics. Beneath the manual are processes that define what gets done, when, where, and by whom. This process documentation includes the cross-functional flowcharts. Beneath the process documentation are work instructions. Work instructions specify in a detailed manner how the process works. The documentation is written in text form and often includes specific graphics to help explain how to do something. Be aware that not all processes need work instructions.

The strategic planning process does not lend itself easily to specific low level instructions. However, many information systems processes such as Backup and Disaster Recovery Management, Installation and Configuration Management, and Security Management do require specific work instructions. Finally, under work instructions, are records. Records provide the evidence that the process was executed and to what extent and quality level. Records are the deepest forms of documentation. In Information Systems, records often take a variety of formats, from electronic files or logs to manually filed paper. Be careful in the selection of what a record is and what is not a record, so as not to get buried in worthless documentation.

There are six steps to creating effective documentation:

1. **Understand Audience and Use:** Obtain an understanding for why the documentation is needed (e.g., training, reference, daily information).
2. **Determine Format:** Determine the best format (e.g., text, flowchart diagrams, drawings, photos). Ensure a consistent format across all processes and work instructions.
3. **Identify Document Requirements:** Do documents need requirements such as unique numbers, effective dates, or revision control?
4. **Create:** Write or draw the documentation.
5. **Proof and Modify:** Check the work. Does it meet the objectives?
6. **Distribute:** Establish a procedure to send documents to users or to locate them in common work areas.

PITFALLS TO AVOID

Pitfalls to avoid when developing the new process:

- **Rushing the development or redesign:** No doubt, by this time in the improvement cycle, somebody is getting impatient. It may be a boss, it may be members of the process improvement team, or it may be you. Somebody will have expected the team to be completed by now, to have implemented a solution, and to be demonstrating results. Do not let these pressures rush the development or redesign effort that needs to be done. Make sure that the expectations are set correctly. Now is the time to focus on the tasks at hand and stay true to the process methodology. Spend time thinking through the new process options and developing the best solution possible. Keep the effort moving forward.

■ **Choosing short-term solutions:** Resist rushing a solution and implementing a short-term solution. Granted, sometimes improvement needs to be incremental and implementing radical change may not feasible. But recognize the importance of designing the process around long-term objectives.

■ **Forgetting the objective:** Most importantly, do not lose sight of the objective. During the brainstorming sessions, ideas and solutions will be created that may not relate to the process objectives outlined in the Case for Action. These solutions are generally innovative, fun, and sometimes irresistible. Remember, keep the process development focused. Process projects have a tendency to creep into something far greater than originally intended. Focus on the objectives and resist this tendency.

■ **Not involving the right people:** Everything we do is dependent upon people. In process improvements, the people involved or touched by a process are many, from operations technicians to managers to executives. Recognize the presence of turf issues and manage them. Involve the right people in the process effort. Foster participation. The best improvements often come from a cross-section of people. Most importantly, involve the customers of the process. Their input in the design of the new process is critical. They will have to live with the results.

■ **Trying to do too much:** Remember that involvement takes time. Not only will the team members be working on these efforts, but they will also be doing their normal jobs. Manage the resources on a process project like any other project. Define the tasks. Set a schedule. Measure the work actually performed.

■ **Not thinking outside the box:** Redesign is a creative process. It requires that the team members approach a problem or create a solution with an open mind. Work to ensure that people recognize the value of creative ideas. Recognize those creative ideas, not only during the redesign session but after as well.

■ **Focusing on technology rather than process:** There will be many suppliers who will want to help fix or improve the process by providing a technology solution. The software and technology demos are impressive and it is easy to quickly become enamored with all of the features and functionality of these new solutions. Do not lose sight of the real process issues. Leverage technology, but do not be swallowed by it. Search and apply solutions that add value.

■ **Defining the problem to fit the solution:** Do not go into the design session with a technology or process in mind and proceed to define the problem to fit the solution. Consider the individual requirements and environment. Keep a focus on the boundaries of the problem.

■ **Oversimplification:** Processes are complex. Do not underestimate the tasks, interrelationships, and considerations that are an everyday part of every process. During the redesign session, decompose activities and tasks to make sure that there is clarity and understanding for what actually needs to get done.

KEY POINTS TO REMEMBER

■ Designing a new and improved process requires a consolidation of process knowledge.

■ Suppliers and customers are instrumental in defining the requirements of a process.

■ Brainstorming is used to eliminate, simplify, separate, combine, and automate process steps.

■ A list of best practices and design components is helpful in designing a new and improved process.

■ Assessing the new design helps to ensure that it meets the factors relative to competing elements, business factors, efficiency and effectiveness, resolving issues, and risk.

■ Appropriate process documentation can assist in keeping the new process alive.

■ Deliverables for step six, Future State, include:
  ■ Brainstorming notes
  ■ Cross-functional flowchart of the new process
  ■ Process documentation (including purpose, owner, metrics, and tools)
  ■ Process procedures

NOTES AND IDEAS FOR MY PROCESS IMPROVEMENT EFFORT

_____

_____

_____

_____

_____

_____

_____

_____

_____

_____

_____

_____

_____

_____

_____

_____

_____

9

IMPLEMENTING PROCESS CHANGES

"You have to stop in order to change direction."

Erich Fromm

The new process is now designed and the organization is eager to proceed. While it is important to move quickly, do not rush. Consider all the ramifications associated with the implementation, including the impact on technology and people. Develop the proper implementation plan for the new process. After implementation, continuously monitor and enhance the new process. A great process poorly executed can be a disaster. Success lies not only in how well the new process is planned, but how well it is carried out. These are the tasks necessary for a successful implementation:

- **Determine Impact of Technology**
- **Determine Impact on People**
  - Change management
  - Define roles, responsibilities, training, and staffing
- **Plan the Implementation**
- **Risk Management**
  - Implementation strategies
  - Implementation plan
- **Implement the New Process**
- **Monitor the Process**
- **Improve the Process (and back to implement, monitor)**

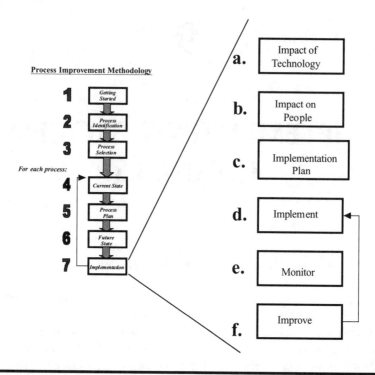

Figure 9.1 Implementation

These tasks are depicted in Figure 9.1.

Throughout this book, the focus has been on processes. However, as we shift our focus to implementing the new process, we need to consider all the aspects of systems management. Systems management is composed of processes, technology, and people. This is depicted in Figure 9.2. As shown by the figure, there is some overlap between processes, technology, and people.

This book has discussed extensively the process element of systems management, but not the elements of technology or people. Let us now look at the impact of these additional elements during the implementation of the new process.

DETERMINE IMPACT OF TECHNOLOGY

Technology can be very overwhelming given the ever expanding number of technology alternatives available. However, many processes can be significantly enhanced with technology. For example, systems management tools such as Tivoli or Computer Associates Universe can automate and significantly impact many processes such as Software Distribution

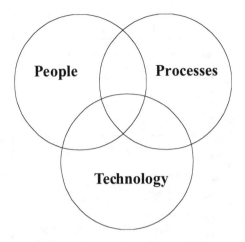

Figure 9.2 Systems Management

Management, Inventory and Asset Management, Problem Management, and Performance and Availability Management. There are also many point solutions that address specific needs such as call tracking software for Problem Management, performance-monitoring tools for Performance and Availability Management, and modeling tools for Capacity and Storage Management Process.

Be aware that one entire process could use several different technologies in its implementation. For example, the technology used in the automation of a Problem Management Process could include:

- **Computer Telephone Integration:** Based on an incoming call, the user hardware and software environment would appear automatically on the Help Desk agent's screen.
- **Call Tracking Application Software:** The agent can record and store the call information for analysis later.
- **Inventory Application Software:** This would facilitate identifying and tracking the particular software and hardware used and reassigning assets and licenses as needed.
- **Knowledge Management Tools:** The agent could diagnose and troubleshoot problems based on prior experiences and solutions.
- **Decision Support Tools:** The agent could analyze call data and identify trends and root issues, such as a lack of training in a particular department or area.

This book is not intended as an evaluation of the hundreds of automation tools available on the market. However, these tools can be

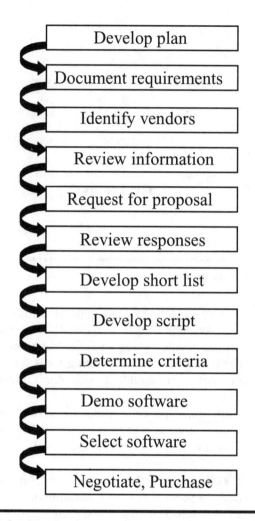

Figure 9.3 Tool Selection Process

extremely valuable and should be evaluated when redesigning a process. Beware that technology can only help an organization improve a process if the technology supports the process and the philosophy to be implemented.

The tools to automate the process are selected as is any other software as outlined in Figure 9.3. General steps to follow are:

1. Form a selection team and develop a project plan
2. Document the requirements
3. Identify possible vendors

4. Obtain information and review a long list of potential packages, eliminating any that do not meet the requirements. Obtain industry evaluations.
5. Send Request for Proposal with requirements for vendor response
6. Review the responses and literature
7. Identify approximately three packages for detailed evaluation
8. Develop detailed script or test cases for demonstration
9. Determine key criteria for rating software
10. Demonstrate the software
11. Select the leading software
12. Negotiate with the vendor

After selecting the technology, go back and update the process map if necessary. The technology may shed new light on ways to improve the process or may require process changes. Although some people may choose to look at technology first before designing the new process, it is important that the process is not too dependent upon the technology, as the technology may change. Also, by looking at technology before thinking through the new process, it can be easy to become enamored with the technology. A temptation may exist to implement the technology even though it may not accurately fit the process. These situations can result in a great technical solution looking for a problem. It is best to first make sure the problem is understood before automating it. Therefore, it can be helpful to first think through the new process before looking at the technology options.

DETERMINE IMPACT ON PEOPLE

The impact on people can be very difficult to manage given individuals' sensitivities to change. It is important to understand and be sensitive to the change management issues that occur during a new process implementation.

Change Management

Change is constant and a natural part of everyone's life. It affects all organizations and can come about in many ways (as shown in Figure 9.4), such as:

■ Mergers, acquisitions, downsizing
■ Organization restructuring and personnel redeployment
■ Increasing customer demands
■ Significant growth

Figure 9.4 Change Is Constant

- Continuous process improvement
- Shifting priorities
- Technology developments

An organization must become skilled in adapting to change. In the book entitled *The Fifth Discipline*, Peter M. Senge explains how to make an organization a learning organization that can adjust to change. A successful leader must understand the change process, communicate the right messages in a timely manner, and understand the impediments to change and how to overcome them. Successful change management requires developing strategies to facilitate the organizational, human, and cultural side of change. More often than not, new processes fail because the organization fails to recognize and manage the human components of the change. In fact, 70 percent of reengineering projects fail because of people and cultural issues.

For almost every process change, there is a corresponding cultural change. Technical people in management roles often forget to give proper attention to the human factors when implementing changes. Changes in an organization are often dramatic and traumatic for some individuals. Change is seldom easy to implement. Typically, an organization cannot be changed without requiring the people to change. Therefore, there needs to be sensitivity to issues that people will have with the transformation and change. Cultural changes are complex and must be taken into account when developing goals, objectives, action plans, roles, and responsibilities. It is critical to bring people along through the process of

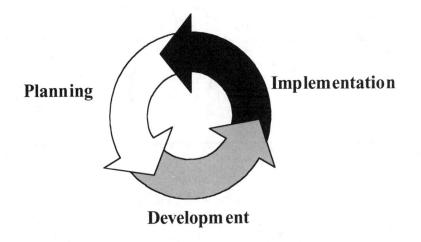

Figure 9.5 Change Process

change. Do not make assumptions that people understand the mission, scope, and their role in the impending change.

A culture that is too structured may have difficulty changing quickly. It needs to be led, and leading takes time. An organization that has an informal culture may have difficulty adding formal processes and procedures. An organization that is changing too fast may have difficulty introducing additional change without stressing the organization. When implementing a new process, consider the culture changes that need to occur to make the implementation successful. For example, do behaviors, thoughts, beliefs, vocabularies need to change? It is important to implement reward systems that support the goals and objectives of a culture to be fostered. Figure 9.5 depicts the phases that an organization goes through during a change.

- **Planning:** Preparing the organization to design and accept that change is necessary
- **Development:** Creating and designing a new environment to close the gap between the current and future state
- **Implementation:** Implementing desired changes, measuring results, and identifying required adjustments that may be necessary

The primary obstacles to successful change include resistance, inadequate team skills, and neglecting the impact of personal issues. Although many organizations consider the impact to the organizational structure, many do not address the personal issues or transitions that occur to the employee. People fear being forced to change. They may be afraid of

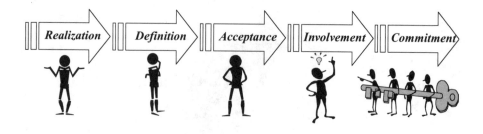

Figure 9.6 Individual Transition Stages

failure or the unknown or frustrated with something new. Change requires individuals to get out of their comfort zone, and individuals often fear the loss of control. Many people do not object to change, but they may object to having change forced upon them without being involved or having an understanding of the benefits of the change.

During the change process, individuals also go through transitional stages as shown in Figure 9.6:

- **Realization:** Becoming aware of the change, understanding the personal impact of change, letting go of the past and realizing change is necessary
- **Definition:** Overcoming anxiety and resistance through additional information, understanding, and training, and identifying the new roles that will be needed
- **Acceptance:** Accepting the new roles and responsibilities, values, and attitudes while seeing the benefits of the changes
- **Involvement:** Becoming supportive of the change and helping it succeed
- **Commitment:** Personally believing in the change and being committed to its success

It is important for the manager to guide individuals through the various stages. The goal is to minimize the negative impact for the person as well as ensure ongoing productivity. To do this, communication about the change is critical. Communication must be continuous, complete, enthusiastic, simple, and honest. Incomplete information will be filled in with speculation, often inaccurate. This is how the uncontrollable grapevines get started. In addition to the formal messages and communication plan, also consider the informal and inadvertent messages that are delivered. People can misinterpret everything that leaders say, or do not say, in times of change and turmoil. The communication program must consider the participants needs at each stage of the change process (e.g., awareness, understanding, training, and inspiration). Also, the various individual learning styles, such as audio, visual, or participatory, need be considered. At the beginning of the change process, ensure that the Case for Action and the vision is communicated to personnel. Stress reasons why the change is necessary, what the change will be, and how the change will occur. Also stress what the change will mean to them. Regular status updates with open discussions of issues, concerns, and problems are critical throughout the process.

In addition to communication, these are additional factors that will help people adjust to change:

- **Direction:** Individuals need to understand a clear objective and purpose for the change. Without the proper direction or vision, individuals will be confused.
- **Rewards:** The reward system must encourage the changes that are to be made. Without the proper incentives to support the change, changes will occur much more slowly.
- **Structure:** The proper management structure, including project management, clear responsibility and authority, and defined tasks, must be in place to monitor and manage the change. Without the proper structure, individuals will be frustrated and unproductive, and the project may experience false starts.
- **Metrics:** Specific measures identify exactly where the organization is, where it is going, and how to know when it has arrived. Without metrics, ambiguity will occur.
- **Leadership:** Someone with a passion for the change must be leading the effort to set the direction and influence others to follow. Without leadership, nothing will happen.
- **Training:** Individuals need to be comfortable with their new roles and responsibilities. They need to have the skills to do the job. Without proper training, individuals will experience anxiety.
- **Resources:** The proper resources must be assigned to accomplish the change. Without sufficient resources, individuals will be frustrated.

Even with good communication and management, people react differently to change. Emotions may include anger, happiness, fear, optimism, anxiety, challenge, resistance, enthusiasm, relief, helplessness, hopefulness, or pessimism. There are also different roles that people assume during the changes.

- **Early risers:** These are the people who thrive on something different and are willing to accept a challenge.

- **Early adapters:** These people recognize that change is about the only constant and are willing to stretch their comfort zone. Early adoption of the change may or may not be what is desired.
- **Pragmatists:** These people want to be shown the benefits of the change. If the benefits cannot be demonstrated to their satisfaction, they will probably become resistors. Many times these are the change survivors who have been in the organization for a long time and have seen many waves or changes in the past. They may be doubtful until they see changes actually happen.
- **Resistors:** These people are very specific in their position and often communicate it in very blunt terms. They strongly resist the change through lack of participation and may even sabotage the effort.

Define Roles, Responsibilities, Training, and Staffing

The new process may have a significant impact on the roles and responsibilities, jobs, and skills of the individuals in the organization. Before actually implementing the new process, do the following steps as shown in Figure 9.7:

1. List the roles and responsibilities necessary to complete the new process. Be sure to consider the impact of any new technology.
2. Group the roles and responsibilities into similar job functions.
3. Map the roles and responsibilities to job titles.
4. Assess any impact to the organization structure. If necessary, develop new organization structure. Assign individuals to jobs.
5. Develop new job descriptions or update existing ones.
6. Identify the training necessary for each person. Training is critical to the success of the new process. Individuals must feel comfortable with the new process and their role in the process.
7. Identify hiring that may be necessary. Make sure the new process has the resources necessary to be successful.

PLAN THE IMPLEMENTATION

Now that we have considered the impact the new process may have on people and technology, we can plan the implementation. A list of considerations to review before implementation follows:

- What is the magnitude of the change?
- How many stakeholders are involved or have an interest in the change? What is the formal and informal power and influence the stakeholders have over the change?

List roles,
responsibilities

Group roles,
responsibilities

Map to job titles

Assess impact

Develop new jobs

Identify training

Identify hiring

Figure 9.7 Changing Jobs

- How many individuals will be impacted by the change? The more people who are impacted by the change, the more communication and planning is necessary. As more employees are impacted by the change, the scope and structure of the implementation changes.
- What is the impact on their primary skill? How much will the new process disrupt the participants?
- How many people will have to learn new skills? The amount of training that is necessary will impact the implementation time.

- How many people will have to change behaviors? The degree of behavioral changes required also impacts the scope and structure of the change.
- How significant are the technology changes that are required?
- How much cross-functional cooperation is required in the new process? The more times a process crosses organizational boundaries, the more communication and teamwork is required, which increases the magnitude of the change.
- What is the timeframe to implement the new process? Do individuals involved feel that adequate time has been provided to accomplish the changes?
- Is there a link between performance results and the change? Will the change have a positive impact on the salary, status, or job of those impacted?
- Are there other parties involved in the new process such as external vendors and consultants?
- Were individuals impacted by the changes involved in the development of the new process?
- Is the organization ready for the change and the new process?
- Is there an agreement regarding the need for change? Do the participants understand why the new process is being implemented?
- Do the individuals have a common vision for the future?
- Do the individuals involved understand what is specifically required of them and what their roles will be in the new process?
- What is the degree of commitment from the stakeholders?
- What is the impact on the culture?
- How much change is the organization experiencing? Organizations can tolerate only so much change.
- What is the history of successful implementations of change? Past success with change can be a large advantage. Likewise, past failures can be an inhibitor. Past changes that resulted in workforce reductions may lead to resistance to subsequent changes.
- What resources are allocated to the new process? The resource commitment plays a key role in the management commitment and resulting success of the change.
- What is the potential for workforce reduction?
- What are the obstacles and risks in the change?

Although these questions may seem daunting, especially when stacked into a list, keep in mind that the intent is to consider the issues before implementation rather than after.

RISK MANAGEMENT

An additional task to be done before implementation is to manage the various areas of risk that were identified when the new process was validated. Effective management involves proactively managing the risks and implementing strategies to deal with the risks. Some of the possible risks with the new process include:

- Availability of resources for implementing the new process
- Availability of resources for the ongoing operation of the process
- Acceptance of the new process by process participants
- Technology risk
- Business issues and risks
- External suppliers or external entities risks

With any new process, there are challenges and risks. Effective risk management can be used to mitigate the impact of the risk. Examples of how risks could impact a new process include:

- Loss of quality of the systems or solutions
- Availability and reliability issues
- Increased costs
- Missed deadlines
- Personnel issues including motivation, training, and turnover
- Failure to meet objectives or metrics
- Customer dissatisfaction
- Technology issues
- Impact to the business

Steps to manage risk include:

- Clearly state the risk so it is understood and can be managed properly. What could go wrong? Identify the cause, condition, and the consequences of the risk.
- Identify who is responsible for managing the risk.
- Identify the probability of the risk happening. This could be a numeric value for high (3), medium (2), or low (1), or it could be a percent likelihood of happening.
- Identify the impact or severity of the risk. This impact could be identified as high (3), medium (2), or low (1).
- Identify the overall exposure of the risk. Multiply the probability times the impact to determine the overall exposure. The risks can be prioritized by the overall exposure. You may choose to ignore

Risk	Responsible	Probability	Impact	Exposure	Prevention Plan	Contingency Plan
IS personnel turnover	Sue Adams	3	1	3	Listen, IS satisfaction survey & actions	New employee training plan
Technology difficult to use	Ben Smith	3	2	6	Test and train in new technology	Evaluate technology options
Technology not working	Ben Smith	1	3	3	Test and train in new technology	Evaluate technology options
Technology not perfect fit for process	Ben Smith	2	2	4	Test and train in new technology	Evaluate technology options
Customers don't like process	Andy Johnson	1	3	3	Communication to customers	Modify process
IS process participants not trained	Sue Adams	1	3	3	Training	Training
IS process participants don't like new process	Sue Adams	2	1	2	Training, communication	Listen, modify process
Lack of resources to implement	Andy Johnson	2	2	4	Management commitment	Modify process
Lack of resources for on-going operation	Andy Johnson	2	3	6	Management commitment	Modify process
Issues with interfaces to other processes	Andy Johnson	2	2	4	Test process	Modify process
Metrics get worse rather than better	Andy Johnson	1	2	2	Pilot	Analyze, modify process
Documentation gets out-of-date	Sue Adams	3	2	6	Periodic review of documentation	Update documentation
Process doesn't work	Andy Johnson	1	3	3	Test process, pilot	Analyze, modify process

Note for probability, impact: high=3, medium=2, low=1

Figure 9.8 Risk Management Example

the risks with low exposure, as they may not be worth the effort to manage.

■ Identify the plans to prevent or minimize the risk.

■ Identify contingency plans if the risk occurs, trigger appropriate action for when it should occur, and decide who is responsible.

An example of these steps is shown in Figure 9.8. In addition, be sure to ensure that the risk management, control, and metrics are integrated into the overall design of the process and understand the amount of change that is necessary to implement the new process.

Implementation Strategies

With the groundwork established, we now have some choices on how to implement the process. There are three implementation strategies:

■ **Implement a pilot:** When the risk is extremely high, consider implementing a pilot portion of the implementation. In essence, a pilot is a test run of the implementation, while the old process continues to operate. If significant technology changes are involved, a pilot implementation can be useful.

■ **Implement in phases:** When the amount of change is great, consider implementing the process in phases to reduce the risk. Phased implementations or versioned releases are an effective method of breaking a large implementation into small, logically coherent, and achievable pieces. The phases or versions support the concept of continuous improvement. The current situation has been identified as well as the future state, with incremental steps to move the organization to the future state. Implementing in phases will also allow response to feedback from each release and is far better than analysis paralysis.

■ **Implement big bang:** This is implementing the entire new process in its entirety and accepting the associated risks.

Implementation Plan

Depending on the scope of the changes involved, it may be advisable to develop an implementation plan, outlining the steps that must be taken for complete implementation. Follow a similar structure to the project plan identified at the beginning of the project.

As part of the implementation, estimate the implementation costs, review impact of the benefits, and update the return on investment that was estimated earlier. Although this may seem redundant, it is critical to begin

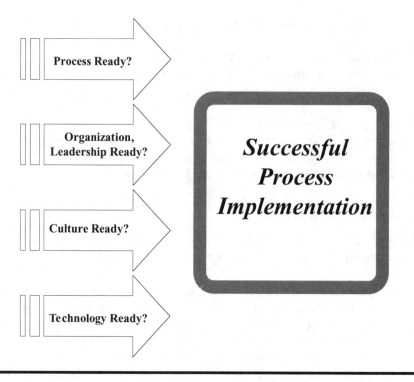

Figure 9.9 Components for Succesful Process Implementation

the implementation with an accurate understanding of the costs that will be incurred. The worst thing that can happen is that after implementation is begun, management realizes that it is going to cost more than anticipated, and the implementation of the new process must be abandoned after a partial implementation. Be sure to include all the estimated costs, including:

- Purchase costs of new technology (hardware and software)
- Ongoing maintenance costs of new technology (hardware and software)
- Costs of retraining personnel
- Travel costs associated with implementing the new process
- Personnel or reorganization costs
- Consulting costs

After having an accurate representation of the return on investment, review all the components to make sure they are ready to implement. As shown in Figure 9.9, the process, organization and leadership, culture, and technology must all be ready to implement. Appendix I is a final checklist to ensure the new process is ready to be implemented.

Success Criteria

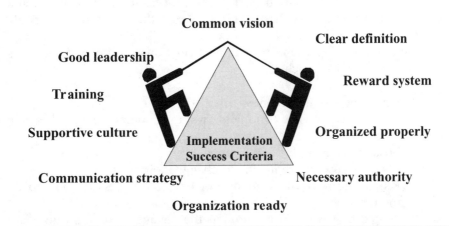

Figure 9.10 Implementation Success Criteria

Following are suggestions in dealing with new process implementations as shown in Figure 9.10.

- Is the organization ready for the change and does it understand the purpose for the change? Consider both the organizations directly impacted by the change as well as those indirectly impacted. The Case for Action must be clear, believable, and understood by everyone.
- Does everyone have a common vision for the new desired state?
- Does good leadership exist that can implement the changes and accept responsibility? The leader must support the change whole-heartedly. Leadership must be direct, involved, and visible. The leader must model the new behavior that is expected.
- Do a communication strategy and plan exist to communicate awareness of the goals and progress toward the goals, as well as to acknowledge success toward achieving the goals?
- Do members have the necessary authority to enact the changes and perform the functions in the new environment?
- Is there a clear and understandable definition of the activities and sequence that must be performed in the newly changed environment?
- Has the culture been considered and will it support the changes?
- Will the organizational design support the changes? Performance management systems must also be appropriate including recruiting, training, measuring, and reward systems.

IMPLEMENT THE NEW PROCESS

Now that the implementation of the new process has been planned and the impact of the changes has been considered, the new process is ready to be implemented.

There are many reasons why implementations are not successful as shown in Figure 9.11, such as:

- Employee morale declines.
- Change is resisted and old ways of doing things become entrenched.
- Business is disrupted significantly.
- People refuse or are unable to change their behavior.
- People are not trained or do not have the necessary tools to do the new job.
- People find ways to get around the change or only portions are accepted.
- It takes too long to implement. People lose interest or opportunities are lost.
- The organization remains in a firefighting mode rather than a planning and process-oriented one.
- Resources are wasted or underestimated.
- The new process is not understood and operates less than efficiently.
- There is significant turnover and loss of confidence in leadership.

These symptoms can usually be traced back to three primary barriers to change:

1. **Lack of support:** Lack of support can be traced back to the vision and the beginning of the process-improvement initiative. Other elements that indicate a lack of support are poor incentives, inadequate resources, and incomplete or ambiguous action plans. If this is the case, go back to the beginning, affirm and communicate the management support. Ensure that proper incentives, resources, and plans are in place to demonstrate the commitment to the effort.
2. **Adaptive capacity:** The ability of the participants in the implementation to adapt to the change may not be high. Many times, individuals may have the desire but not the skills or resources. Reevaluate the timing of the implementation to ensure it is not too much for the organization to handle at the given time. Ensure proper training is in place.

Business disruption   Inefficient process

Not enough resources

Behavior not changed

Morale declines   New process not understood

Too long to implement   Lacking training

Change is resisted   Turnover

Remain in firefighting mode   Go around change

Loss in confidence of leadership

Figure 9.11 Reasons for Implementations to Fail

3. **Ambiguity of the implementation:** This again relates back to the vision and action plan. Both must be clearly stated and effectively communicated to develop a broad understanding of the implementation. If not, add clarity and communication.

MONITOR THE PROCESS

The work does not end once the new process is implemented. Processes degrade quickly, and conditions or requirements may change. Continually monitor and improve the new process. Be sure to regularly review the metrics to measure the success of the new process. Publish and celebrate the progress.

Once a new process has been implemented, a post-mortem must be conducted to provide closure to the implementation and formalize the process of learning from past experience. It is best to wait two to five weeks after the new process is implemented to complete the post-mortem. If results are diagnosed too early, people will focus on the normal implementation difficulties. If a post-mortem is done too late, participants may forget valuable lessons learned during the implementation.

To do a post-mortem on a process improvement effort, it is helpful to assemble those involved and discuss the implementation. Be sure to include the suppliers and customers of the process. Have a skilled, neutral facilitator to moderate the meeting, as emotions may run high. Make it clear that the purpose of the meeting is to identify improvement areas, not to blame or vent. Consider these questions:

- How does the new process function better than the old process?
- How was the implementation of the new process?
- What could have been done better to make the implementation of the new process smoother? Were there warning signs of potential implementation problems?
- What areas need to be improved in the new process? What areas are still struggled with today?
- What are the recommendations for future process improvement efforts? How could the entire process improvement project have been improved?

Be sure that someone publishes notes during the post-mortem discussion, as these will be needed for future process improvement efforts. Make sure that improvement areas that were identified are acted upon. It will be helpful to revisit the notes from the post-mortem after a few months to ensure actions have been taken for all the issues that were identified.

IMPROVE THE PROCESS

As the saying goes, "The road to excellence is always under construction." Process improvement is a never-ending journey. If something needs to be adjusted, go back to the steps in this book and analyze the process to identify improvements. Do not shortcut the steps in a rush to fix the process, as it could end up worse rather than better.

The process must also be continuously monitored and improved as technology and business environments continually change. A process that was deemed a best practice at one time may not be sufficient in the future, as customer expectations increase, business requirements change, and new technology becomes available. For example, several years ago it may have been excellent service to resolve an information systems issue within an hour or two. Today, as businesses become increasingly dependent upon computers and rely on e-business, five-minute responses may be too long. There have been several examples where systems outages have caused a major impact in a company's well being, stock price, profits, and reputation. As processes are improved, what initially excited the users will soon become an expectation, as we have seen with the ever-increasing speed of e-business. Continuous improvement is inevitable and required.

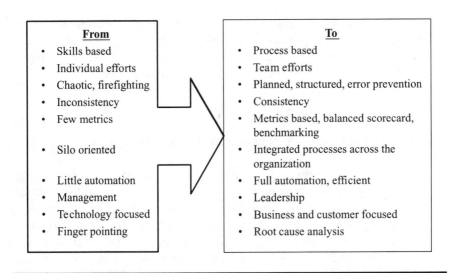

From	To
• Skills based	• Process based
• Individual efforts	• Team efforts
• Chaotic, firefighting	• Planned, structured, error prevention
• Inconsistency	• Consistency
• Few metrics	• Metrics based, balanced scorecard, benchmarking
• Silo oriented	• Integrated processes across the organization
• Little automation	• Full automation, efficient
• Management	• Leadership
• Technology focused	• Business and customer focused
• Finger pointing	• Root cause analysis

Figure 9.12 Information Systems Vision

To keep pace with the changing expectations and requirements, continuous process improvement attitudes must be institutionalized into the culture of an organization. After completing the first process improvement effort, review what has been learned and apply these lessons to the next process improvement effort. Lessons learned may include how to implement a new process; how to deal with cultural, political, and other barriers; and how to increase the ability to learn and implement the new process quickly and effectively. As we continuously improve and move the organization through the process evolution, it may be helpful to create an environment checklist that communicates the vision for where the organization needs to be and where it is currently. This checklist can be updated on an annual basis to see the progress made as an organization toward reaching the goals. An environment checklist is provided in Appendix J. Some components of a world-class environment are shown in Figure 9.12 and include:

■ All customer needs are met with quality systems and solutions on a consistent basis.
■ Benchmarking is done on a regular basis to continually improve processes and metrics.
■ The organization is fully process based, with all procedures and processes well documented and understood.
■ A balanced scorecard may have been developed, with metrics posted regularly and all members striving for improvement.
■ Processes are fully integrated and fully automated.

- Users understand and participate eagerly in the processes.
- Causes of poor performance are eliminated.
- New technology and process improvements are prototyped, piloted, and added to the process on a regular basis.

PITFALLS TO AVOID

In the Implementation step, there are several pitfalls to avoid.

- **Fear of change:** To some extent, everyone has a fear of change. Do not assume that because Information Systems individuals are intelligent they will be willing to change and have no doubts or concerns. The best way to handle fear is through continuous, open, and honest communication. Reassure individuals what their role will be in the new process. Individuals must realize how the new process will benefit them. Be sincere and realistic so that people do not become skeptical. Most fear of change is imaginary, not real.
- **Insufficient training:** Ensure that all personnel fully understand the new process and particularly their roles in the process. Train, train, and train again. Ensure that the new process is fully documented. Do dry runs of how the process will operate once implemented.
- **Lack of understanding of the impact on people and the organization:** Implementation can be a disaster without considering the impact on the people, organization, and culture. These areas take time to adjust to changes. Do not force the process improvement too fast, or disaster can result. Consider the impact on each individual involved in the process. Perhaps job responsibilities will change. Make sure job descriptions, reward mechanisms, training plans, and expectations are updated and communicated fully. Organization changes are often necessary to support the new process. The people side of the equation can cause a perfectly designed process to fail if not attended to properly.
- **Unrealistic time frames:** Implementing change takes time. Although frequently it may feel like a revolution, process improvement must be an evolution of continuous improvement. Particularly if there are people and culture issues, ensure that the schedules are realistic. Remember that realistic targets motivate, while unrealistic targets frustrate.
- **Lack of budget for technology:** Make sure that a realistic budget exists for the process improvement effort. Although some processes can be improved significantly without capital investments, to make

quantum improvements and provide consistency across processes, many of the key processes may require technology that is not already in place. For example, a Problem Management process is much more effective with software for tracking and recording calls, even if it is a simple and basic tool. The process improvement team can lose motivation very quickly if they have been convinced they have authority and responsibility to improve the process, but the first request they bring which requires funds is not approved.

- **Thinking the job is done:** Process improvement is a continuous journey, not a single event that is completed. Continuous improvement is an entire change in culture and focus for the organization. Once a new process is implemented, there are often issues that must be addressed to assure the success of the new process. Seldom is a new process implemented perfectly. More often, it will require continual refinement and improvement.

- **Politics:** At times, hidden and personal agendas can get in the way of improvement, particularly when organizational and responsibility changes are required. Although it is easier to say than do, communication is the key to getting through the political barriers and turf issues. It is critical that the communication is open, honest, and frequent. If organization changes are necessary, make certain everyone understands why the changes are happening and has a clear, defined role. In a political environment, there is often more concern with the *who* rather than the *what*. Focus improvement efforts on the *what*. Ensure that vision, goals, and objectives are clearly understood by everyone and reward mechanisms are changed to support the new behavior. Consider what is right rather than who wants it done. Then, communicate, communicate, and communicate some more. Listen to the issues, determine if they are real, and address the concerns. Just keep moving and do not let improvement efforts get derailed.

- **Insufficient management commitment:** When management commitment and support wanes, it can be very difficult to complete the implementation. This can be a challenge, particularly if insufficient resources are provided to the effort. A word of caution: do not implement a new process unless the proper resources are available to make it successful, even if it means putting the effort on hold. More damage than good can be done by implementing a new process without the support necessary. If this is the case, make sure that management understands the issue, risks, and what is required to make it successful.

KEY POINTS TO REMEMBER

- Before implementing a new process, be sure to consider the impact on people and technology.
- Manage the change process. Consider changes in culture, roles and responsibilities, organization, and individual"s habits. The reward system should support the new expectations.
- Communicate, communicate, and then communicate again!
- Ensure that all individuals are trained.
- Consider implementing large changes in phases or versioned releases.
- The job is not done with the implement ... continuously improve.
- Listen to feedback and conduct a post-mortem.
- Deliverables for step 7, Implementation, include:
  - Process implementation plan
  - Updated job descriptions
  - New process implemented
  - Notes, measures on results
  - Improvement plan

NOTES AND IDEAS FOR MY PROCESS IMPROVEMENT EFFORT

10

SUMMARY

"Imagination is more important than knowledge."

Albert Einstein

METHODOLOGY OVERVIEW

Congratulations! You have now made it through the complete process improvement methodology. Looking back at our journey, we began in the first step by getting the process improvement effort started, putting the plan and vision together, organizing the project team, and conducting training in process improvement. In the second step, process identification, we understood the environment and identified the processes in the environment, their purpose, benefits, and issues. In the third step, we selected the processes for improvement by analyzing the value and prioritizing the processes. For a particular process, the fourth step gathered information on the process, flowcharted the current state of the process, and analyzed the process. In the fifth step, we developed a plan to improve the process that included the process objectives, metrics, baseline and benchmark data, and Case for Action. The sixth step developed the new process, validated it, and developed process documentation. In the seventh step, we determined the impact on technology and people, planned the implementation, implemented the new process, monitored, and made improvements to the process.

The length of time it takes to go through the seven steps will vary considerably from organization to organization. Depending on the resources committed to the effort, many companies find they can pursue multiple process improvement efforts in a parallel fashion.

Figure 10.1 shows a complete snapshot of the seven-step process and the associated activities.

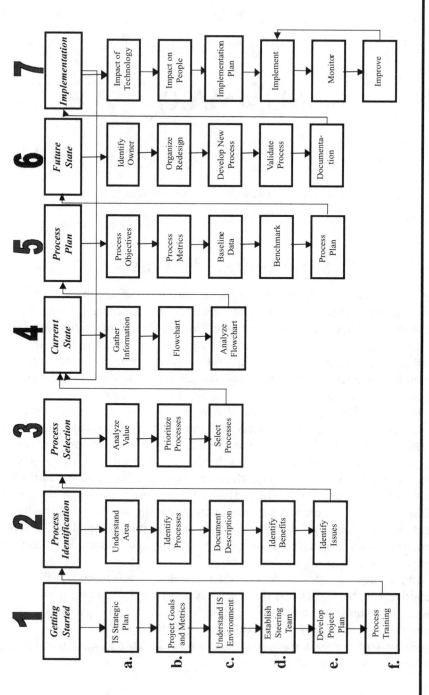

Figure 10.1 Process Improvement Methodology

SUCCESS CRITERIA

As shown by Figure 10.2, there are many components for a successful Information Systems process improvement effort. The criteria for success include:

- **Management commitment and leadership:** Leadership must support the change to the new culture and create the climate for change. Priorities must be rationalized, the organization and resources aligned to make the changes occur. Leadership is necessary to communicate the vision and belief that quality improvements are worth the effort. Leadership is required to make quality improvement in Information Systems a real goal, not just a fad.
- **Values and vision:** A solid vision fuels high performing teams. A clear vision builds trust and cohesion, improves focus, establishes priorities, and assists with decision making. As the saying goes, "If you don't know where you are going, any road will get you there." The group members must understand the vision for the future, the target they are aiming for. Everyone must have a common focus for the activities. The strategic intent and direction of information systems must be aligned with the business direction. The vision for the entire process improvement effort (as outlined in Chapter 3) as well as the vision for the particular process (as outlined in Chapter 7) must be clear. A good vision must be SMART: **S**pecific, **M**easurable, **A**chievable, **R**elevant, and **T**ime-based.
- **Teamwork:** As processes cross the organization, teamwork is an absolutely necessary component for success. Create a knowledge-sharing environment. Everyone must work well as a team. Brainstorming and facilitated sessions allow teams to solve problems together.
- **Culture and rewards:** Goals and incentives must be aligned to support the new goals and process improvement. People do what they are rewarded for. Use rewards to help assure success.
- **Corrective action and feedback:** Feedback encourages learning and root cause analysis. In order to excel, people need to change, learn, and adapt. Aim correction at the root cause, not the symptom. Use early warning systems to detect potential problems before they occur.
- **Error prevention:** Doing the right things right the first time is the basis of total quality management. Unfortunately, in many Information Systems organizations, there is no time to do it right, but always time to do it again. Information Systems organizations are often too busy fixing yesterday's problem to prevent tomorrow's problem. Every

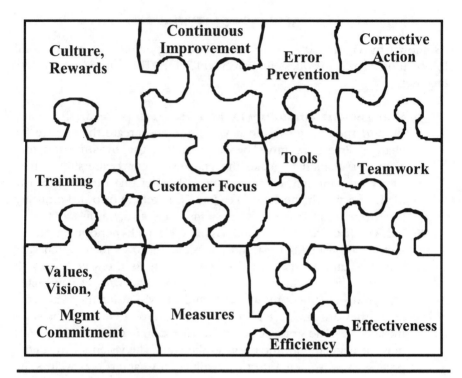

Figure 10.2 Success Criteria

error has a root cause that can be identified and prevented. If problems do occur, direct corrective actions at the root cause not the symptoms. Error-free work can be planned and organized. If time and effort is expended up front, it reduces the time and effort in firefighting to correct an error. Overall, it is less expensive to do things right the first time. This involves an entire culture shift for an organization as it impacts every aspect of work.

- **Continuous improvement:** Quality is a journey, not a destination. We are never done. We never arrive. The more we improve, the more we are aware of the improvements that must be made. Continuous improvement is a way of life. Quality concepts must be integrated into the heart of all processes. Learn new approaches and set new goals.

- **Customer focus:** The customer for an Information Systems organization may be defined as anyone utilizing the information systems services, whether an internal user or external customer. Many technologists forget that the sole reason the Information Systems organization is in existence is to bring value to the customer and the business. Information Systems personnel work with the customer to define quality and agree on the proper trade-off with cost. Although the Information Systems personnel may feel they are doing a tremendous job, it may be completely unacceptable when viewed from the perspective of the customer. Information systems process improvement requires a transition from the silo-centric information systems environment to an integrated, customer-centric environment.

■ **Measures:** Metrics must be explicitly linked to the information systems and business objectives. Take care in deciding what to measure. Measurements must be objective and used to improve the process, not to punish the people. Use customer surveys to regularly measure customer satisfaction.

■ **Tools:** Technology can be a key component in much of the process improvement in an organization. Automate where it makes sense and where there is a solid return on investment. Make sure the processes share a common data model to avoid inaccurate or duplicate information and entry. For example, PC inventory and user information may be necessary for the Inventory and Asset Management Process, Software Distribution Management Process, and the Problem Management Process.

■ **Efficiency:** Be certain that processes are designed for optimum efficiency. Make sure that things are done right the first time, rather than over and over again. Efficient processes allow being responsive and adaptive to changes. Minimize the number of departments and individuals that are involved.

■ **Effectiveness:** Make sure that processes are effective, or doing the right thing. Is the process even necessary at all? Are the desired results achieved? Make sure the right work is being done. With technology changing so rapidly, upon investigation, some of the activities in a process may be found to be totally unnecessary due to updated technology, but the tasks are continuing because they have always been done.

■ **Training:** An organization's success is dependent upon the knowledge, skills, and motivation of the employees. Invest in the development of employees through education, training, and continuous growth.

BENEFITS OF PROCESS IMPROVEMENT

In the past, Information Systems was seen mainly as automating back-office systems and reporting financial data on what happened historically. As systems evolved, and expectations increased, Information Systems departments were required to become more proactive and forward looking. Modeling, forecasting, and other methods became important. As organizations reached out to their customers and suppliers, demands increased on Information Systems to develop systems that touched outside the four walls of the organization, and supply-chain management, sales-force automation, and other applications grew in importance. Today, expectations from information systems are even higher, as companies are looking to technology to provide them with a competitive advantage and market dominance. Internet and e-business technologies are becoming critical for survival.

In most companies today, technology is tightly linked with core business processes. Systems and technology must provide continual reliability and optimum performance for businesses to succeed. As such, information systems processes must be improved or reengineered to be immediate and deliver high levels of availability and satisfaction. Efficient and effective information systems processes are no longer just a competitive advantage; they are a basic requirement to stay in business.

For years, Information Systems organizations have heard complaints that they are not responsive enough to the changing business needs and they see their backlog continually increase. Businesses are tired of spending too much money on technology and projects that never meet business expectations. The only way to change those perceptions is through improved performance. Process improvement is a basic requirement to meet the demands placed on Information Systems organizations today.

The only thing that is certain about our future is that change will continue (and probably accelerate). Advancements in technology as well as shifts in the values and expectations of consumers and businesses have changed the requirements placed on Information Systems. One definition of insanity is doing the same thing over and over again, expecting different results. If we want improvements in quality, customer satisfaction, or speed, we need to change the process. Inaction is not an option in a rapidly changing world. A world-class environment does not come about by itself. It is built by organizations that follow practical, efficient, and effective processes while paying attention to the needs of the customers and the voices of their employees. It is time for Information Systems to change their strategies, philosophies, and culture to become more competitive. Information systems process improvement is the mechanism to become more competitive.

No matter what role we play in an organization, we can have an impact on process improvement in the information systems environment. Each of us can make a difference. Be part of the solution rather than part of the problem! Status quo will no longer be acceptable to meet the challenges of the 21st century. Assess the organization, train and educate the individuals, and begin the process improvement effort. Get out of the firefighting mode. Solve problems once rather than over and over again.

Influence the organization into a new way of operating in Information Systems. By embracing the principles and philosophies of quality management and process improvement, the quality of products and service provided by the Information Systems organization can be improved. We can make a sustained contribution to the success of the company. We now have the knowledge; what can we do to begin the process improvement journey?

KEY POINTS TO REMEMBER

- Continuous management commitment and leadership are required to make quality improvement embedded in the culture rather than a passing fad.
- Everyone must share the vision for the future.
- Quality is everyone's job.
- Root cause analysis, not simply fixing the symptoms, must be practiced.
- Spend the extra effort to do things right the first time.
- Quality is a journey, not a destination.
- Efficient and effective information systems processes are a basic requirement to stay in business.

NOTES AND IDEAS FOR MY PROCESS IMPROVEMENT EFFORT

_____

_____

_____

_____

_____

_____

_____

_____

_____

_____

_____

_____

_____

_____

_____

_____

_____

APPENDICES

A. PROCESS CHARACTERISTICS CHECKLIST

	Strongly Disagree				Strongly Agree

1. Required

- Are the objectives of the process related to the mission and objectives of Information Systems and the business? — 1 2 3 4 5
- Does this process directly support key business functions or processes? — 1 2 3 4 5
- Does the process contribute to the value and quality of services being offered? — 1 2 3 4 5
- Are there business changes that may require changes in the process or emphasis relative to the process? — 1 2 3 4 5
- Would the information systems image suffer if this process were not performed adequately? — 1 2 3 4 5
- Is the process critical to delivering the expected level of availability or satisfaction? — 1 2 3 4 5

2. Defined

- Does the process have a distinct beginning and end? — 1 2 3 4 5
- Is the process fully documented? — 1 2 3 4 5

3. Measurable

- Are the objectives of the process defined in quantifiable terms? — 1 2 3 4 5
- Is the attainment of process objectives measured and monitored on a regular basis? — 1 2 3 4 5

4. Effective

- Is the process defined, thoroughly documented, and understood by all process participants? — 1 2 3 4 5
- Are procedures and standards relative to the process defined, documented, and understood by all process participants? — 1 2 3 4 5

■ Are process objectives, organization responsibilities, procedures, standards, and measurements regularly assessed to ensure process effectiveness?   1 2 3 4 5

■ Is there a minimum number of issues relative to the functioning of the process that must be resolved?   1 2 3 4 5

■ Is user satisfaction (those who receive output from the process) measured regularly?   1 2 3 4 5

5. Efficient

■ Is the process automated with tools?   1 2 3 4 5

■ Is the process optimized to reduce unnecessary interventions?   1 2 3 4 5

■ Has the value of each activity been assessed to ensure it is necessary?   1 2 3 4 5

■ Has the administrative burden been minimized for the process?   1 2 3 4 5

■ Is the process improved on a regular basis?   1 2 3 4 5

■ Have the process activities been measured to reduce workflow times and improve efficiencies?   1 2 3 4 5

■ Is decision time reduced to a minimum throughout the process?   1 2 3 4 5

■ Have personnel requirements been reduced for the process?   1 2 3 4 5

■ Are measurements regularly reviewed on the process?   1 2 3 4 5

6. Adaptable

■ Is the process able to accept new business requirements?   1 2 3 4 5

■ Would a change in personnel significantly impact the functioning of the process?   1 2 3 4 5

■ Are roles and responsibilities well documented?   1 2 3 4 5

■ Are the skill levels of the process participants up to date to allow for changes in the process?   1 2 3 4 5

■ Is the process documentation current and updated?   1 2 3 4 5

7. Owned

- Is responsibility for attaining process objectives throughout the organization assigned to a single accountable individual?   1   2   3   4   5
- Does the process owner have the decision-making authority required to ensure that process objectives are met?   1   2   3   4   5
- Does the process owner have sufficient resources to attain the process objectives?   1   2   3   4   5
- Has the process owner improved the process?   1   2   3   4   5

8. Cross-functional

- Does the process cross organizational boundaries?   1   2   3   4   5
- Are cross-organizational responsibilities for the process defined, documented, and understood throughout the organization?   1   2   3   4   5

9. Feedback loop

- Does a feedback loop exist?   1   2   3   4   5

10. Technology independent

- Would a change in technology significantly impact the process execution?   1   2   3   4   5
- Can new technology be added as necessary?   1   2   3   4   5

B. CUSTOMER SURVEY

No.	TOPIC	QUESTION	RATING Strongly Disagree ... Strongly Agree
1	Tools	The current systems and tools meet the needs of the business.	1 2 3 4 5
2	Information	I have access to the business information I need.	1 2 3 4 5
3	Training	The training and documentation on the systems meets my needs.	1 2 3 4 5
4	Availability	The systems are available and stable.	1 2 3 4 5
5	Interface	I know who to contact in IS when I have an issue.	1 2 3 4 5
6	Support	I am able to get critical problems (e.g., PC and network problems, system not working) resolved quickly. My expectations are to have issues resolved within.	1 2 3 4 5
7	Timeliness	I am able to get IS solutions to business problems (e.g., projects, application changes) in a timely manner. My expectations are to have problems resolved within:	1 2 3 4 5
8	Quality	The quality of the IS solutions and tools meets my needs.	1 2 3 4 5
9	Projects	The IS group delivers projects on time and on budget with the promised results.	1 2 3 4 5
10	Business	People in IS understand the business and the business needs.	1 2 3 4 5
11	Direction	IS has a good strategic direction that is aligned with the business direction and priorities.	1 2 3 4 5
12	Communication	I know what IS is working on, what tools are available and am notified in advance of changes.	1 2 3 4 5

13	Input	I am able to provide input into IS direction and systems as necessary.	1 2 3 4 5
14	Strategy	IS provides a strategic advantage to the business.	1 2 3 4 5
15	Overall	Taking all things into consideration, how would you rate your overall satisfaction with IS?	1 2 3 4 5

16. Strengths — Following are things that IS does very well:

_____

_____

_____

_____

17. Weaknesses — Following are areas that IS should improve:

_____

_____

_____

_____

18. Comments — Additional comments and suggestions:

_____

_____

_____

_____

C. PROCESS EVOLUTION READINESS ASSESSMENT

	Strongly Disagree				Strongly Agree

1. Individuals within the Information Systems organization

- The individuals are willing to change   1 2 3 4 5
- Individuals have a positive "can do" attitude   1 2 3 4 5
- The individuals have a capacity for learning and knowledge   1 2 3 4 5
- There is a lot of teamwork and cross-functional cooperation   1 2 3 4 5
- Individuals are given the opportunity to make decisions and innovate   1 2 3 4 5

2. Information Systems organization

- The information systems group is experiencing pain (could show in the form of turnover, frustration) with the current mode of operation   1 2 3 4 5
- The amount of change the group has experienced in the past year is tolerable   1 2 3 4 5
- The budget which may be necessary exists   1 2 3 4 5
- The resources which may be necessary exists   1 2 3 4 5

3. Business environment

- The pace of business change is rapid   1 2 3 4 5
- The pace of the business cycles is rapid (e.g., sales cycle, manufacturing cycle)   1 2 3 4 5
- The business wants a change from information systems; they are not satisfied with the current mode of operation   1 2 3 4 5

4. Politics and leadership

- The leader is passionate about changing to a process-based environment   1 2 3 4 5

- The leader has a vision of the "to be" environment   1   2   3   4   5
- Individuals who are going to make changes have the necessary authority   1   2   3   4   5
- The leader has the ability to implement reward systems consistent with the new environment   1   2   3   4   5

D. PROJECT SUCCESS ASSESSMENT

	Strongly Disagree				Strongly Agree

Organization

■ Does user management want the project?	1	2	3	4	5
■ Does upper management give its support?	1	2	3	4	5

Project Team

■ Is a project leader/manager assigned?	1	2	3	4	5
■ Has a project sponsor been identified?	1	2	3	4	5
■ Have enough resources been assigned to the project?	1	2	3	4	5
■ Do project team members have the necessary authority?	1	2	3	4	5
■ Are users deciding the business issues?	1	2	3	4	5
■ Are Information Systems individuals deciding the technical issues?	1	2	3	4	5
■ Does everyone understand the business issues?	1	2	3	4	5
■ Do team members have sufficient knowledge?	1	2	3	4	5
■ Have team members been trained?	1	2	3	4	5
■ Is the project manager actively involved and does he or she understand the details of the project?	1	2	3	4	5

Project Plan

■ Is there a formal project plan?	1	2	3	4	5
■ Is there a detailed project schedule?	1	2	3	4	5
■ Do individuals understand their roles and responsibilities?	1	2	3	4	5
■ Are the requirements, goals, objectives, and vision clear?	1	2	3	4	5
■ Is it clear how success will be measured?	1	2	3	4	5
■ Are task estimates realistic? Do they account for vacation, sick, and non-project time?	1	2	3	4	5
■ Are there short-term deliverables?	1	2	3	4	5

- Are tasks structured so it is obvious when they are done?   1 2 3 4 5
- Is one person responsible for each task?   1 2 3 4 5
- Are team members clear about what tasks are assigned and when they are due?   1 2 3 4 5
- Is the budget for the project adequate?   1 2 3 4 5
- Are expectations realistic?   1 2 3 4 5

Project

- Does the project utilize a methodology?   1 2 3 4 5
- Is communication within the project team regular, thorough, and accurate?   1 2 3 4 5
- Is communication outside the project team good?   1 2 3 4 5
- Is the team environment honest, respectful, open, positive, and encouraging of new ideas?   1 2 3 4 5
- Are decisions made in a timely manner?   1 2 3 4 5
- Are there regular reports to management on the status of the project?   1 2 3 4 5
- Is there a methodology to track changes and problems?   1 2 3 4 5
- Are meetings structured and worthwhile?   1 2 3 4 5
- Do control mechanisms exist?   1 2 3 4 5
- Has documentation been completed?   1 2 3 4 5
- Are there weekly progress reports by all team members?   1 2 3 4 5
- Are hours tracked by task and variances reported?   1 2 3 4 5
- Is the technology proven?   1 2 3 4 5

E. PROCESS DESCRIPTIONS

Capacity and Storage Management Process Description

- Defines the quantity, type, and configuration of information systems resources required to support current and projected service levels (e.g., transaction volumes, turnaround times, response times). The level of resources are adequate, but not excessive.
- Monitors, measures, and reports information on capacity of all resources. Examples of resources measured include CPU, memory, disk, tape, network bandwidth, printers, and routers.
- Manages data on various storage technologies (e.g., tape, disk, optical, or paper) to ensure availability, backup, and data integrity and to proactively manage capacity and performance.
- Tunes resources for optimal utilization.
- Predicts, forecasts, and trends future requirements.
- Assesses new technology for performance and cost improvements.

Performance and Availability Management Process Description

- Plans, monitors, measures, reports, and analyzes resource consumption and utilization on a regular basis.
- Measures and reports actual performance and availability results against established service levels. Status and trend reports are created and analyzed for root cause, patterns, critical contributors, or points of potential failures to identify improvements that can be made to meet the targets.
- Interfaces with the Service Level Management Process to determine availability objectives. This includes identifying those transactions and databases that must be available, and when to support the business. The business value or cost of an outage is also determined.
- Identifies actions necessary to improve performance and availability. Improvements may include such things as isolation, concurrency, redundancies, clustering, mirroring, testing environments, and protection from required maintenance windows.
- Proactively models the performance of planned applications, projected future load, and other changes to the environment.
- Optimizes and tunes the use of resources and the configuration for optimal performance and availability.

Change Management Process Description

- Ensures proper evaluation, planning, controlling, coordination, management, execution, and monitoring of any changes made to the production environment while minimizing potential risks and disruption of service.
- Includes changes made to any software, hardware, or procedures including business applications, systems software, network (WAN and LAN), databases, and desktop.
- Changes are documented, reviewed, prioritized, scheduled, coordinated, tracked, reported, implemented, and assessed. All stakeholders who are impacted by the proposed change are informed of the progress of the change.
- Typically handles the majority of changes with a release philosophy. Changes are grouped together to minimize the impact to the production environment.
- Changes may be necessary to resolve problems, prevent problems, handle growth and business changes, accommodate technology changes, or improve performance.
- Also referred to as production turnover.

Backup and Disaster Recovery Management Process Description

- Plans, establishes, performs, and tests the backup and recovery procedures required to restore service for all areas of the Information Systems environment (e.g., LAN, WAN, systems software, business applications, and databases) in the event of a failure, outage, or disaster.
- Ensures that environment and services are restored and business is continued in the event of a system failure, component failure, or a major catastrophe. Includes the activities that both business users and information systems individuals must perform to bring the environment back to functioning status.
- Includes the evaluation and selection of a cold site, warm site, or hot site.
- Assures that recovery is performed within the established service level requirements.

Problem Management Process Description

- Detects, reports, documents, analyzes, diagnoses, corrects, and monitors problems impacting information systems services.

- Root problems are determined to proactively prevent problems from recurring and causing future disruption of service.
- Problems are prioritized through severity analysis.
- Establishes a single point of contact for all issues.
- Problems can occur through events, calls, or requests by users.
- Problems can occur end-to-end, that is in business applications software, systems software, network (WAN and LAN), databases, hardware (server or desktop), or procedures.
- Includes first level support (taking the call and initial problem solving), second level support (detailed problem solving), and third level support (in depth problem solving and vendor interface).
- Also referred to as call management, event management, help-desk management, and request management.

Installation and Configuration Management Process Description

- Includes configuration identification, configuration control, configuration auditing, and status accounting.
- Provides physical and logical configuration information to support all components.
- Identifies information that must be maintained, establishes the system to maintain the information, collects the information, and reports the information.
- Coordinates the installation tasks of any changes or additions to hardware and software. This includes planning, coordinating subcontractors, and coordinating product delivery notification to all affected parties.
- Physical implementation of hardware and software components. This includes coordinating with the change process, testing, turnover, and post implementation review.
- Manages the connectivity between all components, including hardware, software, and network to guarantee reliability and that service level agreements are met.
- Coordinates with the change control process to manage all changes to the infrastructure as well as with the problem management process to manage any issues that may occur as a result of changes.
- Determines proper naming conventions.

Schedule Management Process Description

- Plans, defines, documents, executes, and monitors processes which run, taking into account predefined relationships and dependencies among the processes.

- Coordinates any schedule changes that may be necessary with the Change Management process. Also, coordinates with the back-up and recovery process to execute the proper back-up processes as necessary.
- Establishes and executes proper back-out and recovery actions in the event of process failure.

Software Distribution Management Process Description

- Plans, installs, tests, and distributes software to designated platforms, including servers, desktops, and notebooks.
- Coordinates with the Inventory and Asset Management Process to maintain an inventory of software. Also interfaces with the Change Management and Configuration Management Processes.
- Maintains master versions and copies of all software.
- Communicates all software changes and trains users as necessary.
- Ensures compatibility of software components.
- Determines standard software releases.

Understand Requirements Process Description

- Understands, develops, documents, and obtains agreement on the business Case for Action and the business need.
- Identifies, defines, and documents the specific project requirements and deliverables.

Design Solutions Process Description

- Translates the business requirements to specific designs.
- Plans the development of the solution.

Construct and Integrate Solutions Process Description

- Acquires, builds, customizes, and integrates solutions to create the solution to meet the design and business requirements specifications.

Test Solutions Process Description

- Develops test plans, details test cases, performs the test, and analyzes and documents the test results.
- Includes unit testing, system testing, integration testing, and stress or performance testing.

Customer Acceptance Process Description

- Assures that the customer is satisfied with the solution.
- Includes user training, final acceptance testing, and development of user procedures and documentation.

Understand Business Needs Process Description

- Understands the business.
- Proactively identifies how IS can utilize technology to assist the business.
- Identifies business needs and potential IS projects or requests.

Market IS Offerings Process Description

- Communicates to the customers what IS services and capabilities are available. Includes new employee training as well as on-going information on projects and changes (through reports, intranet communication, etc.).

Service Level Management Process Description

- Plans for a specific level of service and then manages and monitors to ensure the satisfactory delivery of the services.
- Negotiates, establishes, approves, documents, reports, reviews, and monitors service level agreements.
- Service level agreements may include service hours, availability, throughput, support levels, responsiveness, restrictions, functionality, contingency, security, and costs.

Customer Satisfaction Management Process Description

- Manages the business relationship and expectations with customers.
- Obtains regular feedback of customer satisfaction.
- Communicates on a regular basis (e.g., newsletters, status reports, intranet pages) with customers so they understand the activities of IS and status of projects.

Facilities Management Process Description

- Manages the facilities required to provide the environment for equipment and personnel.

- Makes certain that services and proper protection are in place, such as UPS and physical security.

Financial Management Process Description

- Plans, identifies, monitors, and controls the costs (or potential revenues) associated with IS.
- Includes the capital and expense budget.
- Manages financial lease/rental arrangements, all spending, vendor payments, and hardware and software maintenance.
- Determines and manages any charge backs that may exist.
- Communicates to users the cost of IS services.
- Communicates costs to the IS organization and instills a culture of cost management.

Vendor Management Process Description

- Manages the review, selection, and on-going relationship with vendors through the entire life cycle. Includes hardware, software, and service providers.
- Includes vendor selection, acquisition, negotiating and maintaining contracts, tracking orders, processing payments, and monitoring quality and service level.

IS Strategic Planning Process Description

- Works with business management (all levels) to determine the information systems direction and architecture for the future.
- Establishes a governing body, such as an IS Steering Committee, to establish priorities and decisions.
- Identifies the business direction and business case, as well as the resulting architecture requirements for people/organization, IS processes, technical infrastructure, and business application environment.
- Prioritizes IS projects and efforts.

Security Management Process Description

- Designs, executes, and monitors the security procedures and policies for the protection, confidentiality, and integrity of IS assets.
- Designs network and system components to provide a secure environment. Includes firewalls, virus protection, etc.
- Monitors and controls access to the network, systems, and data.
- Reports all unauthorized attempts to access the system.

Inventory and Asset Management Process Description

- Identifies, tracks, and reports all IS resources (hardware, network, and software) through their complete life cycle from acquisition to management, maintenance, and disposal. Includes tracking information such as location, user, version, serial number, and date of acquisition.
- Includes tracking, reporting, and auditing of software licenses to guarantee software license compliance, as well as training and communication to make certain all employees understand software license compliance issues.

Human Resources Management Process Description

- Plans, establishes, and reviews the organizational structure.
- Identifies jobs, roles and responsibilities, and job descriptions.
- Assures that proper incentives are in place to reward employees.
- Documents, evaluates, and communicates employee performance against established goals and objectives.
- Creates and maintains a positive work environment that promotes teamwork, change, and growth.
- Communicates to the IS organization so the objectives and direction of the business and IS are understood.

F. PROCESS BENEFITS

Capacity and Storage Management Process Benefits

- Allows Information Systems to be more proactive and less reactive.
- Reduces risk of problems caused by lack of capacity.
- Increases ability to maximize current investments.
- Improves efficiency, reduces cost through improved utilization.
- Improves relationship with the business.
- Allows for better acquisition with advanced notification of needs.
- Reduces negative impact to users.

Performance and Availability Management Process Benefits

- Manages Information Systems resources to meet a specific target.
- Increases quality due to controls in place.
- Improves cost efficiency.
- Lessens firefighting and creates more proactive management.
- Reduces impact to end users and disruptions.
- Supplies data for vendor service level negotiations.

Change Management Process Benefits

- Increases quality of changes as more individuals review the change and provide input.
- Improves planning, communication, and coordination regarding the change.
- Reduces the chances of impacting systems availability and the need for backing out changes.
- Provides higher user and Information Systems productivity due to less disruption.
- Identifies the cost and increases the visibility of changes.
- Restrains the introduction of nonessential changes.

Backup and Disaster Recovery Management Process Benefits

- Allows the recovery of services for business continuation.
- Lessens disruption to the business.
- Provides consistent and reliable services to the business.

Problem Management Process Benefits

- Increases productivity in the business as the impact of problems is minimized through timely resolution.
- Prevents problems or quickly resolves them by using information from previous occurrences.
- Improves relationship between the business and Information Systems; this is the main contact the users have with Information Systems.
- Resolves the most severe problems or those with significant impact to the business first.
- Provides feedback on the success or failure of changes that are implemented.

Installation and Configuration Management Process Benefits

- Improves control of information systems assets and changes to hardware and software.
- Increases system availability and performance.
- Improves change management and control.
- Improves problem management.
- Improves ability to support contingency and disaster planning.

Schedule Management Process Benefits

- Maintains efficient operation of jobs.
- Lessens disruption to business as issues are resolved quickly and accurately.
- Provides business with information to manage the business.

Software Distribution Management Process Benefits

- Improves the quality of software, reduces errors.
- Minimizes the impact of changes on end users.
- Ensures software is safe, secure, and controlled.
- Assures consistent and compatible software is used.
- Reduces problems Information Systems must resolve as all users are on consistent releases.
- Reduces chances of software piracy and use of illegal software.
- Reduces risk to the organization.

Understand Requirements Process Benefits

- Guarantees that the true business requirements are met.
- Identifies ways for technology to assist the business.
- Improves relationship with the business.
- Improves quality of solutions.

Design Solutions Process Benefits

- Provides documented design that can be reviewed and approved by Information Systems and the users.
- Reduces development costs and rework.
- Decreases development time.
- Ensures complete understanding of business issues before development begins.
- Improves quality of solutions.

Construct and Integrate Solutions Process Benefits

- Improves quality of solutions.
- Develops solutions to meet the business needs.
- Decreases development time.
- Decreases errors.

Test Solutions Benefits

- Increases quality and reduces errors.
- Reduces impact to business.

Customer Acceptance Process Benefits

- Increases user satisfaction.
- Makes sure users are trained properly.
- Reduces problems with trained users and proper procedures.
- Improves relationship with the business.
- Increases Information Systems satisfaction in meeting users requirements.

Understand Business Needs Process Benefits

- Identifies ways for the business to use technology for a competitive advantage.

- Improves relationship with the business.
- Increases Information Systems' understanding of the business.

Market IS Offerings Process Benefits

- Ensures existing resources are utilized.
- Increases user satisfaction.
- Improves relationship with the business.

Service Level Management Process Benefits

- Reaches agreement upon expectations with the business users.
- Minimizes unreasonable demands on services.
- Helps to clearly understand the user requirements.
- Helps achieve a specific, consistent, and measurable level of service.
- Balances the desired service level with the associated costs.
- Increases user productivity and minimizes the impact to users.
- Measures the progress of improvements in availability and other areas required to achieve user satisfaction.
- Improves the relationship with the business and Information Systems.
- Communicates consistent objectives.
- Facilitates the development of a customer service-oriented culture.

Customer Satisfaction Management Process Benefits

- Improves relationship with the business.
- Improves customer satisfaction.
- Provides metric to measure and enhance progress.

Facilities Management Process Benefits

- Assures most efficient and effective utilization of resources and facilities.
- Reduces costs.

Financial Management Process Benefits

- Ensures spending is aligned with business objectives.
- Allows business decisions to be made about options available for information systems services.
- Establishes targets and monitors costs against budgets.

- Prioritizes spending.
- Increases understanding of the impact on services of budget reductions.
- Builds business Case for Action justifying expenditures.
- Makes sure business sponsorship exists for Information Systems investments.

Vendor Management Process Benefits

- Decreases costs.
- Improves vendor relationship.
- Ensures and improves vendor quality.

IS Strategic Planning Process Benefits

- Provides effective and efficient management and allocation of information systems resources.
- Improves communication between business and Information Systems organization.
- Links the Information Systems direction to the business direction.
- Plans the flow of information and processes.
- Reduces the time and expense of the Information Systems life cycle.

Security Management Process Benefits

- Ensures valuable resources and company information are protected and secure.
- Reduces risk to the organization.

Inventory and Asset Management Process Benefits

- Reduces costs to the organization with knowledge and control of assets.
- Reduces risk to the organization with software license compliance.
- Improves utilization of assets.

Human Resources Management Process Benefits

- Increases Information Systems employees' satisfaction.
- Reduces turnover within Information Systems.
- Assures roles, responsibilities, and objectives are clear.
- Improves efficiency and effectiveness of the Information Systems organization.
- Makes the Information Systems organization feel a part of the business.

G. POSSIBLE PROCESS ISSUES

Capacity and Storage Management Process Issues

- Additional capacity and storage is acquired as needed rather than through proactive planning.
- Projections and models only account for the current system with incremental volume changes and do not account for new applications that are planned.
- No regular process in place to review and delete unnecessary files.
- Resources tuned to the maximum with no capability to achieve improvements without additional expenditures.
- Capacity not projected consistently in all areas (e.g., WAN, LAN, mainframe, and servers).
- Unreliable information for business on future workload projections.
- User service levels expectations are unrealistic.
- End-to-end information not available.
- Lack of automated tools.

Performance and Availability Management Process Issues

- Planned applications are not modeled to proactively review the impact on performance.
- Availability is not measured or managed end to end.
- Lack of modeling capabilities.
- Lack of automated tools.
- Difficult to do.
- Dependence on suppliers and vendor quality.

Change Management Process Issues

- Administrative bottlenecks and approvals slow the process.
- May not be used for all changes, whether to business applications, network, systems software, desktop, hardware, software, or procedures.
- May not use the process consistently.
- May not be flexible for quick response or emergency fixes.
- Changes not done in a release philosophy.
- Incomplete reporting of changes along with associated problems.
- Lack of documented standards, service levels, and consistent criteria.
- Lack of automation, manual paper-based process.

- Overly rigid process with unnecessary overhead and bottlenecks.
- Treating all changes with same amount of risk.

Backup and Disaster Recovery Management Process Issues

- A formal disaster recovery plan does not exist.
- A copy of the disaster recovery plan is not stored off-site.
- The disaster recovery plan does not include all components, such as hardware, software, network, and user procedures.
- Backups are not tested.
- Disaster recovery not tested on a regular basis.
- Lack of management commitment.
- Ignorance as to the importance.

Problem Management Process Issues

- Calls are handled inconsistently depending on the skill level of the help desk agent.
- Established process not utilized consistently.
- Users go right to a preferred individual.
- People do not know where to call for help.
- Minimal reporting of data and metrics.
- No formal escalation process.
- User departments grow their own Help Desks to resolve issues more efficiently.
- Problems are resolved on the surface without determining their root cause.
- No formal agreed upon service level requirements.
- Users not happy with the speed of resolution.
- Lack of automation in process.

Installation and Configuration Management Process Issues

- Systems all manual rather than utilizing automated tools.
- Changes done quickly, bypassing the process.
- Configuration captured at the wrong level of detail.
- Process not able to accommodate emergences and quick changes that may be necessary.
- Sufficient staff not allocated.
- May be viewed as unnecessary.

Schedule Management Process Issues

- Procedures not up to date on all jobs.
- Change management process not followed on all changes and documentation not getting updated properly for each job.

Software Distribution Management Process Issues

- Users bypassing the process.
- No test and staging environment used.
- No automated tools used.
- Not all systems using consistent releases or software.
- Process not capable of handling emergencies or quick fixes.
- Unsynchronized releases across distributed environments.

Understanding Requirements Process Issues

- Not taking the time to thoroughly understand the business needs.
- Lack of communication between the business and Information Systems.
- No process in place.

Design Solutions Process Issues

- No process in place, up to the abilities of the assigned individuals.
- Skip this step and go directly to development.
- Incomplete specifications.
- Lack of tools and automation.
- "Not invented here" syndrome.
- Trap to constantly build custom solutions, because "we're different."
- Tendency to change the code to fit the business processes rather than changing the process.

Construct and Integrate Solutions Process Issues

- No consistent process.
- Focus on technical rather than business needs.
- Incomplete unit testing.
- Lack of standards.
- Not re-using code developed elsewhere.

Test Solutions Process Issues

- Incomplete testing to rush to implementation.
- Lack of stress testing and projecting impact on system.
- Incomplete integration testing.
- Lack of tools and automation.

Customer Acceptance Process Issues

- Tendency to skip this step and rush to implementation.
- Often skip user training, or incomplete user training.
- Often skip updating or developing user procedures and documentation.
- Do not listen to user comments.

Understand Business Needs Process Issues

- Often this process is skipped completely.
- No connection with the business.

Market IS Offerings Process Issues

- Frequently, this process is skipped completely.

Service Level Management Process Issues

- Measures may be perceived as too formal, not needed.
- Difficult to develop.
- No automated systems for collecting data to report on service level.
- Agreeing on over-ambitious targets before obtaining valid data on current status.
- Service level measure may be too aggressive, not allowing for changes and preventive maintenance activities.

Customer Satisfaction Management Process Issues

- Often this process is skipped completely.
- Do not make improvements after obtaining input.
- Not followed regularly.

Facilities Management Process Issues

- Lack of proper services and protection in place for all areas (e.g., UPS and physical security).
- Firefighting mode rather than proactive planning by facilities.

Financial Management Process Issues

- Inflexible budgeting process to accommodate midyear changes.
- A budget that does not correlate to the Information Systems and business objectives and strategies.
- No automated tools to easily view and analyze the budget and actual figures.
- Budget determined by setting a target without working through the detailed requirements first.
- Arbitrary budget cuts done before analyzing impact.
- User plans not coordinated with Information Systems budget.
- Lack of business commitment and perceiving Information Systems as an overhead cost function rather than as a strategic asset.

Vendor Management Process Issues

- Always trying to win over the vendors rather than achieving a win-win relationship.
- Not allocating enough time for vendor selection and negotiation.
- Not obtaining input from all necessary areas for vendor selection and negotiations.
- No formal process used consistently.

IS Strategic Planning Process Issues

- No formal process exists.
- Not involving the business; results in inability to obtain approval, no business ownership.
- Not letting the business direction drive the information systems direction. Results in a technical direction looking for a business problem or solving the wrong problem.
- Level too high; not providing a detailed prioritized road map of projects.
- Takes too long.
- Does not result in changes to the direction; results in a book on the shelf.

Security Management Process Issues

- Unauthorized attempts (and perhaps successful attempts) to get into the system jeopardizing the integrity of Information Systems assets.
- No one reviewing the reports of unauthorized attempts.
- Proper automation not implemented (e.g., firewalls, virus protection).
- No management commitment.

Inventory and Asset Management Process Issues

- Assets disappearing.
- Not compliant with software license requirements.
- No knowledge of assets.

Human Resources Management Process Issues

- High turnover in Information Systems.
- Dissatisfied and frustrated Information Systems employees.
- Unclear roles and responsibilities; duplication of effort and some things not getting done.
- No clear objectives and direction for Information Systems.
- Lack of teamwork.
- Lack of feeling a part of the business direction.
- Job descriptions are not current or reflective of actual job responsibilities.
- Career paths are not clear or documented.
- Performance reviews are not done, done late, or not consistent across the organization.
- Salaries are not consistent with the marketplace.

H. PROCESS DESIGN COMPONENTS

Capacity Management and Storage Management Process Components

Planning

- System, network, and media utilization is projected on a regular basis (e.g., quarterly) for future requirements.
- Future capacity requirements including system, network, media, and personnel are planned to meet the future service level requirements. This includes production, development, and testing.
- An overall plan exists for system/network/media with a specific utilization and response rate considered.
- Long-term business plans and projected business volumes are translated into systems requirements and are consistent with projected system/network/media capacity.
- On a regular basis, business application owners provide input on planned business growth that will impact system/network/media capacity.
- Acquisitions are planned and approved based on the capacity projections.
- Response time objectives have been agreed to with the business.
- Automated tools are used to model and forecast future loads.

Reporting

- System, network, and media (tape, disk) utilization is reported and analyzed on a regular basis. Analysis includes peak period, average, and by shift.
- Management reports or queries, which include an analysis of projected versus actual capacity requirements with recommended changes to meet future capacity plans, are reviewed and discussed on a regular basis.
- Response time performance is reported on a regular basis.

Performance and Availability Management Process Components

Planning

- Availability and performance objectives are determined that are required to meet the agreed upon service level objectives.
- Availability and performance objectives are agreed to and documented for systems, applications, and end-user groups.
- Availability and performance objectives are determined by business criticality.

- Objectives have been communicated throughout the organization (business and information systems).
- There are procedures that allow for scheduled outage of systems and applications (e.g., maintenance, enhancements, new release, and changes). These scheduled outages are factored into the objectives.
- Interfaces with the Service Level Management process to determine the service objectives and availability goals.

Monitoring and Reporting

- Availability and performance levels are measured for systems, applications, and end-user groups.
- Availability and performance measures include end-to-end metrics, which measure the true end user availability rather than just CPU.
- Both subjective and objective ratings are collected and compared.
- Regular detailed and summary service level reports are prepared for IS and business management including trend analysis reports.
- Periodic review meetings are held to review service level trends and determine future actions.
- There are documented escalation procedures to follow for service level exceptions.
- User satisfaction surveys are conducted on a regular basis (e.g., annually).
- One person is accountable for the achievement of service levels on a daily basis.
- The actual availability and service level measures consistently fall within the service level agreements.
- Automated tools are used for measuring availability.
- Availability reports are produced and reviewed on a daily, weekly, monthly basis.
- Availability meetings are organized and productive.
- Vehicles and processes exist on a regular basis for users to communicate availability concerns and issues. Escalation process is also available.

Improving

- Trend analysis is performed, including the various components (system hardware, system software, network hardware, network software, application software, client procedures, scheduled outages, environment, people).

- Each outage is reviewed in detail with root cause analysis and reporting.
- Interfaces with the Change Management process in the event that changes are required to improve performance and availability.

Change Management Process Components

Planning

- Policies and procedures are established. Approval levels are established, and roles and responsibilities are defined. Reporting is defined, escalation process identified, quality criteria established, lead times established, and a communication plan developed.
- A release philosophy is used to move changes into production. This includes hardware, system software, desktop, network, and application changes.
- There is a documented process for prioritization of all changes.

Administration

- Changes are recorded, scheduled, assessed, approved, and closed. Back-out and recovery plans are determined, and parties are notified. The overall impact of the change is assessed, including doing a risk assessment. The implementation time is estimated and the change is verified for compliance to standards.
- There is one person responsible and capable as the focal point for coordinating and tracking all changes. That person has the responsibility of interfacing with the application development and systems groups to ensure effective and efficient communications regarding changes.
- All application, network, and system changes are subject to change control and tracking. This includes hardware, software, procedural, and facilities changes.
- For every change there is a consistent change request document in use that includes a description of the change, prerequisite/co-requisite changes, appropriate authorization, and requested date of implementation.
- There is a change log maintained that reflects the current status and history of all changes.
- There is a single published calendar or schedule maintained for all changes.
- A risk assessment is completed for proposed changes to evaluate the test and back-out procedures and assess the impact on availability and performance.
- Management approval is required from all affected areas prior to the implementation of a change.

- There is an automated change management system.
- There is a documented communication procedure for communication of all changes.
- All changes are tested as appropriate.
- Interfaces with the Asset Management process to identify impacted areas.

Execution
- Changes are distributed, installed, activated, documented, validated, and backed-out if necessary.
- Interfaces to the Problem Management process if problems result from the change. Also interfaces with the Service Level Management process in the event that service levels are impacted by the change.

Reporting and Tracking
- Reporting is completed to analyze the effectiveness of the changes.
- Measurements are developed and reported including the number of successful and unsuccessful changes per month by category and a trend analysis of the rate of change.
- Corrective action plans are developed resulting from poor measurements.
- Changes are tracked for success or failure. Problems are linked back to changes.

Backup and Disaster Recovery Management Process Components

Planning
- All key business applications have been prioritized according to criticality to the business.
- Manual data and source documents have been analyzed to establish methods for backup, storage, and recovery.
- A backup of the disaster recovery documentation is stored off-site.
- Backup files are stored off-site.

Testing and Execution
- The recovery process and procedures have been tested on a regular basis (both on-site and off-site recovery).
- Backups of all key files regardless of media (e.g., disk, tape, and manual) are taken on a regular basis. This includes server and user or client information.
- Backup files are tested on a regular basis.
- Appropriate technology is implemented to improve fault tolerance, prevent disasters, and minimize recovery time (e.g., backup generator, emergency lighting, mirroring, RAID, and clustering).

- All critical hardware components are connected to a UPS.
- A virus protection plan is documented and virus detection software is used. (Note: According to a Gartner Group report, viruses can take up to 14 person hours to lessen from a network and cause 4 hours of downtime for each infected machine. An organization with 1,000 computers is expected to encounter at least seven infections over a 12-month period. A proper virus protection plan and tools lessen the risk of infections and provide a means to more quickly recover when an infection occurs.)

Documentation and Reporting

- Recovery procedures are documented and up to date for all business applications, network, systems, and desktop environments.
- Disaster recovery/business continuation documentation exists and is up to date for all business applications, network, systems, and desktop environments.
- Documentation is developed resulting from the testing of recovery plan, including the number, frequency, and length of recovery tests.
- The disaster recovery documentation includes all vendor and employee phone numbers, emergency team formation and communication, contract information, hardware and software configuration information, and alternate site set-up information.

Problem Management Process Components

Call Management

- All hardware (server, LAN, WAN), software (business application and systems software), procedural, and facilities problems are reported, logged, and tracked.
- *All* calls and problems are recorded.
- There is a single focal point for the coordination of all problems.
- There is an escalation process identified when problems are not resolved within established time frames.
- There is a documented method for prioritization severity of problems.
- There is an automated problem management system or tool for tracking calls and problems.
- An automated inventory system is available as the problem is reported. (Note: Up to 50 percent of each Help Desk call can be spent on understanding the hardware and software configuration. Providing access to the inventory data at the time of the call can reduce the time of the call.)

- Calls and problems are consolidated to a central location for economies of scale and ease of use.
- Problems are handled from a variety of sources such as phone calls, voice mails, e-mails, system generated, or Intranet.
- All problems are managed to resolution. The customer is contacted for determination of proper resolution.
- Interfaces with the Asset Management process to obtain inventory information. Interfaces with the Service Level Management to identify impact to service levels. Interfaces with the Change Management process in the event a problem requires a change request.

Analyzing and Resolving

- All problems are reviewed with the root cause determined, fixed, and documented.
- Documented problem determination procedures are used for all problem determination.
- Tools and procedures for proactive systems management are in place.
- Automated problem resolution software and aids are used.
- The impact as well as the duration of problems is minimized.

Tracking and Reporting

- Performance and problem indicators are monitored regularly.
- Trends are analyzed to predict and avoid future problems.
- A problem reporting document or vehicle is used which includes the problem description, severity level, outage information, person reporting the problem, person assigned to the problem, unique problem number, time and date problem occurred, and description of action or resolution of problem.
- A problem log is maintained that contains current and historical problems.
- Problem review meetings are held regularly (e.g., weekly).
- Measurements, which include the number and cause of all problems with duration, are collected and reported regularly.
- Common (high frequency) problems are tracked and reviewed for solutions on a regular basis.
- Service level metrics for problem reporting are captured and reviewed on a regular basis. This includes average/peak call volume per day/week, average/peak time call is open, abandon call rate, percent of calls completed on first call, and average/peak time for call to be solved.

- User satisfaction on problem calls is tracked and reported on a regular basis.

Installation and Configuration Management Process Components

- There are documented procedures for network and systems management.
- There is an up-to-date network configuration chart and systems documentation.
- Automated systems management tools are used as needed.
- There is a separate test system (e.g., CPU or partition) to test systems changes.
- Systems and network software is up to date and upgraded as necessary.
- Systems software is documented, including maintenance level, software release, and date installed.
- There is a single person responsible for tracking and implementing systems and network updates or changes.
- The change management process is used for all systems or network changes.
- All systems and network changes are tested thoroughly before implementation.
- DASD are clearly labeled and match configuration diagrams and documentation.
- Servers are consolidated where it makes sense for efficiency and ease of maintenance.
- The architecture is designed for scalability and flexibility to meet the changing business requirements.

Schedule Management Process Components

- Thorough, complete, and up-to-date operations procedures and documentation exists for each job including backup and recovery instructions.
- Operations procedures and documentation are updated in the Change Management Process.
- Data center personnel are properly trained in the operation of jobs and schedules.
- There is one focal person in the data center that a given user can contact regarding production jobs.
- Service levels have been defined, agreed to, and communicated.
- There is a single, effective automated job scheduling system.

- The data center has input early in the application development cycle.
- Checkpoint/restart is automated wherever possible.
- Jobs contain restartable job steps.
- All rerun time is identified, monitored, and managed to a reasonable level.
- Critical jobs are analyzed regularly to ensure efficiency in processing time and throughput.
- There is a single problem-reporting system that records all problems.
- The data center provides regular reporting, metrics, and feedback on key performance indicators and trends to management, the business application, and systems areas. This includes number of reruns and work bottlenecks.
- The data center has approval authority in the Change Management Process.
- The Problem Management Process is utilized for all problems.

Software Distribution Management Process Components

Planning

- The software distribution process interfaces with the Change Management process so that all dependencies are coordinated. It also interfaces with the Inventory and Asset Management process to obtain accurate inventory information.
- A release plan, pilot plan, and distribution route are defined.
- Given software releases are proactively planned for the year with fixed release dates rather than reacting to every change. It is then decided what changes will be done with each release depending on the readiness of the change.
- Education and training is planned.
- A version and release number is assigned to the software so that issues can be tracked and the software identified.
- A process should be designed to react quickly to system fixes that may be necessary.
- After software is tested and released, no more changes can be done.
- Capacity planning is done in advance to consider the distribution route the software has to take, transfer time, network and line capacity, alternative options, and disk capacity.

Packaging

- Brings the software and system changes in a format that can be implemented.

- Scripts and utilities are used to automate the installation process (unattended).
- Installation prerequisites are checked.

Testing

- The distribution and installation of the software is tested in a simulated environment emulating production as closely as possible.
- Unit testing and integration testing is performed on all software impacted.
- A pilot installation is performed.
- A test report is created and the software is certified for distribution.
- An application owner is identified for each software release for clear responsibility.
- If possible, all combinations of the target environment should be tested. If not possible to do all, a representative sample should be tested.

Distributing

- Physically moves the software package and all supporting data to the installation point.
- The distribution is done in either a push method, where the distribution is initiated and controlled centrally, or a pull method, where it is initiated by the distribution client, or a combination of the two methods.
- Mobile clients are also considered for software distribution.

Installing

- Installs the files and applies any necessary changes to the client system.
- Error levels are checked after every task, and roll back is performed in the event of errors.

Verifying

- Validates the installation was successful or triggers action in the event of failure.
- Reports status information, including pending, executing, successful, failed, or not available.

Understand Solution Requirements Process Components

- Each project has clear and documented business objectives.
- Each project has a clear and documented business case with quantified benefits.

- Dates are not committed until input is received from all parties involved in the development process.
- Each project has an identified user sponsor.
- Project requirements and deliverables are clearly documented.
- Project budget is sufficient to cover all costs.
- Project responsibilities are defined, documented, and agreed to.

Design Solutions Process Components

- Design documentation is developed and kept up to date.
- The design meets the business requirements and has been reviewed by the users.
- Project team members have sufficient knowledge of the business function.

Construct and Integrate Solutions Process Components

- A formal systems development process is documented, up to date, and followed for all projects.
- Each project has schedules with date commitments for tasks less than one week in duration.
- Each project has users identified to provide support and testing.
- Each project has the appropriate amount of executive support.
- Vendor business application packages are kept current.
- All modifications to vendor business application packages are documented, including date, location, and purpose.

Test Solutions Process Components

- Unit testing is performed for all systems and changes.
- Integration testing is performed for all systems and changes.
- Stress testing is performed to simulate the impact to servers and network before major implementations.
- Test cases and test plans are documented.
- Results from tests are documented and reported, including failure rate measurements.

Customer Acceptance Process Components

- All users involved in utilizing the system or change are properly trained before implementation.
- Regular user training is provided, with user certification. Training is one of the most important ways to increase productivity and reduce information systems support costs. (Note: According to a

Gartner Group report, over 30 percent of the total cost of ownership can be improved by proper training programs.)

- Up-to-date and understandable end user documentation is created for all systems or changes.
- End users have approval authority before a system or change is implemented in production.
- After each project implementation, a post-mortem review is completed to identify gaps in meeting the customer requirements.

Understand Business Needs Process Components

- IT has a close relationship with the business.
- IT proactively identifies ways to utilize technology to provide the business with a competitive advantage.

Market IT Offerings Process Components

- New employee documentation and training is available that outlines the information systems tools and services available.
- Regular (e.g., monthly) status reports, newsletters, and other communication regarding Information Systems activities are sent to all employees and management.

Service Level Management Process Components

Service Level Planning

- Translates user requirements into a service level agreement.
- Service level agreements are developed jointly with IS and the customers. The customers define the level of support they are willing to pay for.
- The service level agreement includes a definition of the customer, the roles and responsibilities of IS and the customer, and an outline of the objectives, which are tied to business value when possible.
- The agreement identifies the services provided as well as specific metrics, reporting, and escalation procedures.
- Service level agreements provided include the depth of service to be provided; anticipated user volume, hours of operation; the specific coverage to be provided for hardware, software, and application environments; and specific products supported and not supported. It outlines the customer and caller responsibilities, methods of contact (e.g., phone, fax, e-mail, pager) during prime hours and off hours, response times, and pricing or chargeback methods. It specifies call tracking and reporting processes, data

retention and backup requirements, problem handling, and escalation processes.

- Priority and service level agreements should be based on the impact to the business.
- The agreement defines the review process, failure, and the corresponding consequences.

Service Level Monitoring

- Manages and monitors the services provided to verify that the services fall within the standards established in the service level agreements.
- Key metrics are identified which add value to the business. The metrics could be a balanced scorecard approach, but should include customer satisfaction metrics, technical metrics, and quality metrics.
- Reporting identified should include the specific reports, audience, frequency, and format. When possible, use Intranet delivery vehicles and graphical representations.
- Any exceptions to the agreed upon service level should be identified with the reason for failure and actions taken to correct the issues.
- Escalation procedures outline the steps if problems are not resolved as stated in the service level agreement. Action should be outlined for specific incidences as well as cumulative service level agreements not met over a longer period of time.
- Interfaces with the Problem Management and Change Management processes to provide service level agreement targets, issues impacting the service, and actions taken. Interfaces with the Asset Management process to tie the service level with the asset and track issues.

Customer Satisfaction Management Process Components

- Regular (e.g., annual) customer satisfaction surveys are completed.
- Survey results are analyzed and communicated, and action is taken.

Facilities Management Process Components

- Environment monitors for the data center are calibrated and monitored on a regular basis.
- The circuit breaker information for the data center is documented.
- Facilities information is included in the disaster recovery documentation.

Financial Management Process Components

Budgeting

- The decision is made either to budget all Information Systems assets within Information Systems to make the most efficient use of assets or to manage Information Systems assets by user department to obtain maximum accountability.
- All Information Systems services, assets, personnel, projects, and expenses are budgeted on an annual basis. Obsolescence and depreciation are also budgeted.
- Prior years' expense detail is reviewed before determining the budget for next year; however, all planned expenditures must be justified, not just increases over prior year.
- Information Systems budget expenditures are tied to the business direction and objectives or specific business projects. The budget is used to question the value of services delivered in the eyes of the customer.
- The budgeting process obtains input from all Information Systems individuals as well as all user groups served.
- Outsourcing and partnerships are considered as alternatives during the budgeting process.
- The cost of all requests is estimated and the information is provided to the requesting user and budgeted if justified. Planned noninfrastructure expenditures are evaluated based on return on investment to the business.
- Desktops and other technology infrastructure items are cycled and budgeted as appropriate to reduce maintenance expenses. The total cost of ownership is considered in all budgeting and spending decisions. Information Systems is also able to budget and invest in technology infrastructure up front to eliminate costly upgrades down the road as undersizing CPUs, DASD, printers, and other assets can incur additional expenses.
- Chargebacks or allocations are determined and managed.
- The customer impact and impact on service level of budget cuts or cost reductions are analyzed and communicated.

Acquisition and Spending

- The expenditure and capital approval process is designed for clear and timely decision making and authority. Proper approval levels for spending are documented and followed consistently. A flexible process is used to accommodate unplanned expenditures.
- Payments are matched with purchase requests and budgeted line items.

- Depreciation, capital, and operating leases are reviewed and understood. Purchase and lease options are investigated and analyzed as appropriate.
- IS expenses are not shifted to functional departments to avoid the true IS costs. All Information Systems costs are consolidated and reviewed.
- A system is established to track all Information Systems project costs.
- Spending trends are reviewed on a regular basis. Expected numbers are adjusted regularly.

Reporting and Analysis

- All expenditures (expense and capital) are recorded and reported on a regular basis (e.g., monthly, quarterly, annually). Actual to budget performance is reported and compared. Analysis of expense reports is based on exceptions, and variances are reviewed in detail.
- A key set of financial metrics is established, monitored, and communicated to the organization on a regular basis. Industry and benchmark information is obtained on key financial measures.

Vendor Management Process Components

- Capital expenditures of computer hardware and software are tracked and documented.
- Purchasing of all hardware and software is centralized through one focal point to leverage savings through volume license and purchase agreements.
- The centralized purchasing process is used consistently.
- Volume license and purchase agreements are documented and communicated.
- At least three bids are received for major purchase agreements.
- There is a documented standard list of software and hardware available for acquisition that is adhered to.
- There is a documented list of approved or certified suppliers.
- Supplier performance and quality delivery statistics are prepared and reviewed on a regular basis.

IS Strategic Planning Process Components

- There is a documented and up-to-date IS strategic plan. A process is in place to keep the plan updated regularly rather than treating planning as an event.
- Business management (executive and line) is involved in the development, approval, and maintenance of the IS strategic plan.

- The IS strategic plan includes the business objectives and strategies. A complete business plan exists that identifies the business mission, values, priorities, strengths, weaknesses, opportunities, and threats.
- The high-level Information Systems direction is identified (e.g., vision, mission, objectives, and architecture).
- The plan includes the direction for business applications, technical infrastructure, people/organization, and information systems processes.
- The current information systems situation is documented and understood by business and Information Systems management.
- Strengths and weaknesses (both business and information systems) have been identified.
- Opportunities to assist the business are identified.
- Threats are identified with actions to prepare.
- Competitors' information systems situation is understood and documented.
- The strategic plan includes a business case justification with options available for major projects and changes.
- Projects are tied to high-level objectives and business objectives.
- Detailed information systems projects are identified, prioritized, and scheduled.
- The budget is tied to the projects and is believable.
- The management team is on board and supportive of the direction and changes.

Security Management Process Components

- The security procedures are documented and up to date.
- There is a strong management commitment to compliance of security procedures.
- There is a security classification to identify the appropriate level of authority granted to data and programs.
- Owners are assigned to each group of data, with clear roles and responsibilities documented for the owner.
- A business risk analysis has been performed to identify security exposures.
- Security violations are reported and reviewed on a regular basis, with action taken as necessary.
- There is a focal point or person responsible to control and monitor security and audit compliance, plans, and procedures.
- Appropriate firewalls are designed to protect the network from external risk.
- Virus detection software is run as necessary.

Inventory and Asset Management Process Components

Acquisition

- Controls are in place to prevent the installation of software without going through the proper acquisition and change management processes.
- There is a documented list of standard software and hardware that is adhered to.
- There is a defined and documented need for the acquisition, including options, total estimated costs, anticipated cost savings, and business priority.

Management and Maintenance

- There is a complete and up-to-date inventory of all hardware and software. This includes the entire environment, such as desktops, servers, and network.
- The inventory includes demographic information, such as the person responsible, location, and organization.
- The inventory includes product information such as vendor, version, release, serial number, maintenance, license, value, and cost.
- Information is updated as the asset changes (or moves) throughout the life cycle.
- Asset information is reported and reviewed on a regular basis.
- The inventory information is validated for accuracy throughout the process, such as in the Problem Management process when issues are reported.
- Interfaces with the Problem Management process to provide asset information used during root cause analysis. Interfaces with the Change Management process to identify assets that may be impacted by changes. Interfaces with the Service Level Management process to track service data.
- Automated tools are used for inventory of hardware and software. (Note: Nonautomated inventories are 20 percent inaccurate on average, resulting in misstatements within accounting and incorrect tax reporting.)

Human Resources Management Process Components

Recruitment and hiring

- Employees are recruited through effective and efficient methods.
- Interviewing prospective employees includes multiple input, background checks, and skills rating.

Training

- Comprehensive new employee orientation and mentoring are provided.
- The integration of new employees and new skill sets is encouraged in the Information Systems organization.
- A skills inventory is documented.
- A formal training plan is prepared and updated regularly (e.g., annually) for each employee.
- The skill set required to meet the Information Systems direction is assessed against the current skill set of the group. Necessary training and recruitment plans are established.
- Employees are exposed to and allowed time to explore new experiences, interests, and emerging technologies.
- Crosstraining and backup are ensured for all key positions.

Employee well-being

- Information Systems employees are aware of the business and its direction through regular updates (e.g., monthly, quarterly, annually).
- Employee satisfaction is monitored on an ongoing basis with corrective action taken as necessary.
- Formal surveys are conducted, reviewed, and acted upon on a regular basis.
- Management engages with employees on a daily basis.

Job descriptions

- Job descriptions are documented, up to date, and accurately reflect each job function.
- Responsibilities, requirements, skills, and qualifications are clearly defined and documented for each position.
- An up-to-date organization chart exists, including names, titles, and reporting relationships.

Career paths

- Available career paths are documented and communicated.
- A formal documented career plan exists for each employee.

Performance reviews

- Regular (e.g., annually) performance review appraisals are documented, signed, and retained.
- For performance reviews of all employees and managers, 360-degree input is obtained from managers, peers, employees, and customers.
- Performance issues are dealt with immediately.

Salary reviews

- Salary structures are documented and utilized to ensure salaries commensurate with job responsibilities and performance.
- A regular salary survey is performed to compare Information Systems salary structures against market salary data.
- Individual performance and salary reviews are evaluated along with the value the employee provides the business.
- Incentives are identified to reward performance. Incentive criteria is communicated and documented.

Terminations

- Exit interviews are performed and acted upon.
- Turnover is planned for.

I. PROCESS IMPLEMENTATION READINESS ASSESSMENT

1. Process

	Strongly Disagree			Strongly Agree	
■ The new process has been defined and documented in sufficient detail.	1	2	3	4	5
■ There is a common vision as to how the new process will function.	1	2	3	4	5
■ Metrics have been identified for the process with methods to collect data.	1	2	3	4	5
■ A process owner has been identified to own the process from beginning to end.	1	2	3	4	5
■ Roles and responsibilities are clear, understood, and documented.	1	2	3	4	5
■ A contingency plan has been designed in the event of issues.	1	2	3	4	5
■ Risks have been assessed with mitigation plans identified.	1	2	3	4	5
■ Procedures and standards have been developed to support the new process.	1	2	3	4	5
■ There is a defined customer feedback loop to identify and address any issues.	1	2	3	4	5
■ The time frame to implement the process is sufficient.	1	2	3	4	5
■ The new process is designed for maximum efficiency and effectiveness.	1	2	3	4	5
■ Process is designed for error prevention, doing it right the first time.	1	2	3	4	5
■ Process is designed for root cause analysis.	1	2	3	4	5

2. Organization and Leadership

	Strongly Disagree			Strongly Agree	
■ The organization is ready and motivated for the change.	1	2	3	4	5
■ The organization understands the purpose for the change.	1	2	3	4	5
■ The organization has a common vision for the desired state.	1	2	3	4	5
■ Leadership has been identified to be responsible for the changes.	1	2	3	4	5
■ Management is committed to the change.	1	2	3	4	5
■ A communication plan exists.	1	2	3	4	5

- Individuals have been trained in their new functions.   1 2 3 4 5
- Job descriptions have been updated to reflect the new responsibilities.   1 2 3 4 5
- The organizational design will support the new changes.   1 2 3 4 5
- Recruiting and training mechanisms have been changed as necessary.   1 2 3 4 5
- The proper amount of resources has been assigned to implement the new process.   1 2 3 4 5

3. Culture

- The culture will support the changes.   1 2 3 4 5
- Reward mechanisms have been changed to reflect the desired behavior and metrics.   1 2 3 4 5
- There is trust, honesty, and integrity in the environment.   1 2 3 4 5
- Mistakes are not punished.   1 2 3 4 5
- There is a team atmosphere.   1 2 3 4 5
- Everyone impacted by the change has been considered (including external entities).   1 2 3 4 5
- Behavior changes that will be required have been identified and communicated.   1 2 3 4 5
- Continuous improvement is part of the culture.   1 2 3 4 5
- Focus is on customer satisfaction.   1 2 3 4 5

4. Technology

- The process has been automated with tools.   1 2 3 4 5
- The new technology has been sufficiently tested.   1 2 3 4 5
- Process documentation has been modified to reflect the tools.   1 2 3 4 5

J. INFORMATION SYSTEMS ENVIRONMENT CHECKLIST

1. Management Perspective

	Strongly Disagree				Strongly Agree

- Service level requirements are defined with the users. — 1 2 3 4 5
- Service level requirements are met. — 1 2 3 4 5
- Information Systems proactively provides support. — 1 2 3 4 5
- Information Systems delivers strategic business value. — 1 2 3 4 5
- Information Systems delivers vendor-supported standard packages rather than custom solutions. — 1 2 3 4 5
- Information Systems develops proactive solutions based on a clear understanding of the root cause of problems and the associated implications of the solution rather than reactive solutions. — 1 2 3 4 5
- A balanced IS scorecard is used based on the IS goals and objectives. — 1 2 3 4 5
- Accountability with proper authority is given to individuals for each objective. — 1 2 3 4 5
- Internal processes are defined and documented. — 1 2 3 4 5
- Metrics are used to measure the efficiency and effectiveness of processes. — 1 2 3 4 5
- Metrics are reviewed against goals on a regular basis to drive improvements. — 1 2 3 4 5
- There is strong executive management support for Information Systems. — 1 2 3 4 5
- Expectations are properly managed. — 1 2 3 4 5
- Time frames provided are realistic. — 1 2 3 4 5
- Projects are implemented on time and on budget with the expected business functionality. — 1 2 3 4 5
- Projects are properly planned with small project milestones. — 1 2 3 4 5
- There is a clear and consistent Information Systems vision and objectives communicated. — 1 2 3 4 5
- Priorities are clear and consistent. — 1 2 3 4 5
- Information Systems create future opportunities for the organization. — 1 2 3 4 5

■ Information Systems management directly, visibly, and actively supports performance improvement.   1 2 3 4 5

■ Information Systems management provides clear values and directions. Goals and plans have clear, measurable objectives.   1 2 3 4 5

■ Information Systems management provides a strong customer focus and commitment to learning.   1 2 3 4 5

■ Information Systems management is easy to reach and has regular contact with employees, users, and suppliers on values and performance improvement issues.   1 2 3 4 5

■ Performance expectations are effectively communicated and reinforced on a regular basis.   1 2 3 4 5

■ Long-term directions and expectations are not compromised to meet short-term demands.   1 2 3 4 5

■ Performance reviews include 360-degree feedback including input from users, peers, and management.   1 2 3 4 5

■ Policies and practices reflect commitment to regulatory, legal, and ethical compliance.   1 2 3 4 5

■ A formal consistent process is used to develop an information systems strategic plan that is aligned with the business plan.   1 2 3 4 5

■ Action plans are tracked and monitored against the goals.   1 2 3 4 5

■ User problems are handled quickly and almost always settled by the first person receiving them. It is a regular practice to track, rate, and improve customer service.   1 2 3 4 5

■ Benchmarking is done against world-class organizations.   1 2 3 4 5

■ Processes are continually improved.   1 2 3 4 5

■ Emphasis is placed on problem prevention.   1 2 3 4 5

2. Business Perspective

■ Information Systems is a true business partner with the business units.   1 2 3 4 5

■ Information Systems is viewed by the business as a revenue enabler rather than as an overhead expense.   1 2 3 4 5

- Projects are begun only with a formal business
case in place.   1 2 3 4 5
- A business leader sponsors each project.   1 2 3 4 5
- Complete business requirements are under-
stood before a technical solution is developed.   1 2 3 4 5
- Each project is audited to ensure the business
benefits were achieved.   1 2 3 4 5
- Users are active participants on projects.   1 2 3 4 5
- Information Systems resources understand the
business.   1 2 3 4 5
- A clear business vision as well as business
objectives and priorities is communicated.   1 2 3 4 5
- A formal process is in place to listen to all
customers or users to understand requirements and improve processes.   1 2 3 4 5
- Regular communication flows between Information Systems and the business.   1 2 3 4 5
- Business solutions are designed to meet or
exceed the business requirements.   1 2 3 4 5

3. Organizational Perspective

- Employees freely provide input into the decision-making process.   1 2 3 4 5
- Employees feel empowered so they can
respond quickly.   1 2 3 4 5
- Employees take ownership of projects.   1 2 3 4 5
- Employees are encouraged to be innovative.   1 2 3 4 5
- Information Systems is a team-oriented organization.   1 2 3 4 5
- Communication flows throughout the organization.   1 2 3 4 5
- Information Systems relies on external
resources to complement and transfer knowledge to the existing employees.   1 2 3 4 5
- Career progression is based on a demonstrated
growth in capability and skill.   1 2 3 4 5
- A formal skills development and training program
exists with pre-established skill requirements.   1 2 3 4 5
- Resource allocations are flexible as teams are
created to support specific business initiatives.   1 2 3 4 5

- Resources are aligned by process rather than by function. 1 2 3 4 5
- Resources include technical specialists as well as business generalists. 1 2 3 4 5
- Resources have up-to-date technology skills. 1 2 3 4 5
- Resources are trained in a variety of areas rather than specialized in a narrow function. 1 2 3 4 5
- The organization is flat and responsive to the business requirements. 1 2 3 4 5
- A belief in continuous improvement, innovation, and learning exists in all employees throughout the organization. 1 2 3 4 5
- Reward systems (compensation and recognition) support that belief and performance related to goals. 1 2 3 4 5
- A safe and healthy work environment is provided. 1 2 3 4 5
- Employees are developed to use their full potential and utilized in areas of their strength. 1 2 3 4 5
- Benefits are provided to ensure employees are motivated and justly compensated. 1 2 3 4 5
- Employee satisfaction is polled on a regular basis and actions taken as necessary. 1 2 3 4 5

4. Technical Perspective

- Information Systems implements proven technology to enable business and process change, but is also innovative to proactively address the requirements. 1 2 3 4 5
- The infrastructure is integrated to minimize redundancy in technology, data, and applications. 1 2 3 4 5
- The infrastructure is automated to reduce costs and enable proactive service and support. 1 2 3 4 5
- The infrastructure is simplified and standardized to reduce costs and improve support. 1 2 3 4 5
- Systems and data are centralized or distributed to optimize performance while minimizing systems administration responsibilities. 1 2 3 4 5
- Transactional data is consolidated to reduce user redundancy and input while improving accuracy. 1 2 3 4 5

- Solutions are scalable to accommodate changing business requirements.   1 2 3 4 5
- Legacy systems and infrastructure are replaced as necessary to meet the business requirements and minimize support costs.   1 2 3 4 5
- The information architecture is built to support business knowledge necessary to make the business decisions.   1 2 3 4 5
- The data collected is complete, reliable, timely, accurate, and useful.   1 2 3 4 5
- There is quick and easy access to information.   1 2 3 4 5

REFERENCES

CenterLine Software, Inc. CenterLine Software, Cambridge, MA, 1996.

Gartner Group, "Best Practices List," *Interpose*, Gartner, Stamford, CT, 1997.

META Group. IT Performance Engineering and Measurement Strategies, Meta Group, Stamford, CT, 1999.

Paulk, Mark C., Curtis, Bill, Chrissis, Mary Beth, and Weber, Charles V. "The Capability Maturity Model of Software," Carnegie Mellon University, Pittsburgh, PA, 1991.

Senge, Peter M. *The Fifth Discipline: The Art and Practice of The Learning Organization,* Currency Doubleday, New York, 1990.

The Standish Group International, Inc. "Will Your Project Survive," *CIO Magazine,* February 15, 1999, p. 42.

Stikeleather, Jim. "Insane Expectations," *Computerworld Client/Server Journal,* November 1995.

Strassmann, Paul. "Quality Is the Answer to the Labor 'Crisis,'" *Computerworld,* June 8, 1998.

AFTERWORD

For additional information, contact Strategic Computing Directions at:

952-226-4620
or
acassidy@strategiccomputing.com

Strategic Computing Directions, Incorporated is an executive information systems consulting organization dedicated to providing practical and proven solutions to information systems challenges. The focus of the organization includes:

- Strategic planning and e-business strategy development to identify how to use technology for a competitive advantage
- Current information systems assessment to identify the areas of risk and improvement in an organization
- Information systems process re-engineering to improve the efficiency and effectiveness of an organization.
- Major software and hardware selection and implementation to assist in implementing the strategic direction.

We look forward to the opportunity to assist you on your journey toward building world class information systems that provide companies with a competitive advantage.

INDEX